Family History on CD

Stuart A. Raymond

Published by the
Federation of Family History Societies
(Publications) Ltd.,
Units 15-16, Chesham Industrial Centre,
Oram Street, Bury, Lancashire, BL9 6EN

In association with:
S.A. & M.J.Raymond,
P.O.Box 35, Exeter, EX1 3YZ

First published 2001

ISBN: 1 86006 142 7 (FFHS (Publications) Ltd)
ISBN: 1 899668 18 7 (S.A. & M.J.Raymond)
ISSN 1033-2065

Printed and bound by
The Alden Group, Oxford and Northampton

Introduction

It has been my intention to compile a listing of genealogical CDs for a number of years now, but I thought it best to wait until more were available, in order to make the exercise worthwhile. I did not anticipate a book of this length! An astonishing number of CDs are now available, making it much easier to obtain information without having to travel long distances.

Geographically, this listing includes CDs published throughout the world relating to the British Isles. The latter term includes England, Scotland, Wales and Ireland, as well as the offshore islands. The term 'family history' has been interpreted widely, and there are many items listed here which are likely to be of interest to the local historian. I have also included a number of items on $3\frac{1}{2}''$ floppy discs. I have not however, included genealogical programs.

Arrangement of this listing is by publisher; however, there are extensive indexes of subjects and placenames, and also briefer indexes of authors and surnames. These indexes provide the means to identify the titles being sought.

The great majority of the CDs available are copies of books, most of which are out of print. Parish registers which have already been transcribed and published are very popular with CD publishers; so are trade directories of the 19th century. In some instances two or even three different publishers have produced CD versions of the same book, e.g. most of Phillimore's marriage registers are available in different versions (despite the fact that some of them are of very dubious quality). I hope that the present work will prevent further duplication of effort - although it may be that apparent duplication reflects the fact that particular CDs have been produced in cooperation between different publishers. Very few CDs contain direct copies of original manuscripts; only a handful contain material created specifically for CD publication.

Most publishers are commercial organisations or private individuals, although a handful of genealogical societies and organizations have also issued CDs. The latter include the Federation of Family History Societies and the Latter-Day Saints, both of whom have issued CDs of vital importance for all genealogists.

This volume has been compiled by means of a questionnaire sent to publishers - and therefore suffers from the faults of inconsistency common to such volumes. Accurate bibliographic citations are simply not to be had without checking all the actual CDs oneself - an impossible task, especially given the fact that no library has more than a small proportion of the items cited here. In a few cases, I have been able to verify the dates of original publication from other sources, although this is difficult where several editions of the same book are available, and it is not clear which one has been used. Authors have only been identified when this information has been supplied by publishers. For this volume, I have not attempted to verify other bibliographic information, especially in view of the fact that titles of CDs may be different from the actual titles of the books they contain.

Accurate citations for many of the original books copied may be found in the other volumes of my *British Genealogical library guides,* especially the county volumes, which ought to be checked for relevant material. If you identify a CD listed here that is relevant to you, and which is a copy of a book, you should check to see whether a library near you holds a copy of the original book before you purchase the CD. Most of the books copied for genealogical CDs are to be found in libraries world-wide (although trade directories are an exception to this general rule).

Prices are as reported by publishers; where possible I have indicated postal charges. You should be aware that these prices are liable to change, and that neither I, nor the Federation of Family History Societies, are to be held responsible for such changes.

Virtually all CDs will run on Windows 95 or 98; most will also run on the Mac. I have indicated system requirements in a few instances where they are unusual; however, I would recommend you to check system requirements with publishers before purchase.

This volume may be kept up to date by reference to the CD listings in journals such as *Family tree magazine* and the *Genealogists' magazine,* backruns of which were consulted to identify relevant publishers. Publishers' web sites may also be checked for new titles (and for system requirements). I have indicated some titles as 'forthcoming', but many more are likely to be published after this book has gone to press, and before you use it.

CDs listed here should generally be obtained direct from their publishers. A few are also available from the Society of Genealogists, and a handful of the publishers listed here also stock CDs from a few other publishers, e.g. S & N. There does not appear to be a CD equivalent to the general bookseller.

If you are an assiduous researcher, and you come across items which ought to be listed here, please let me know.

This book has been typed by Cynthia Hanson, and seen through the press by Bob Boyd. Thanks are due to them, to the officers of the Federation of Family History Societies, and to my wife and family. Without the support of all of these people, this book would not have seen the light of day.

Stuart A. Raymond

ABC-Clio, Ltd

35A, Great Clarendon Street, Oxford, OX2 6AT.
Phone: (01865) 311350
Fax: (01865) 311358
Email: marketing@abc-clio.ltd.uk
Web-page: www.abc-clio.com

Agents: Avero Publications Ltd., 20, Great North Road, Newcastle-upon-Tyne, NE2 4PS.
Phone: (191) 2615790
Fax: (191) 2611209
Email: nstc@newcastle.ac.uk
nstc@ncl.ac.uk

Prices

Prices quoted are for personal research editions only. Please inquire for institutional prices.

The biography database 1680-1830. 5 CDs (in progress).
Personal research edition £91.38 per CD (inc. p&p & VAT).

CD1 contents:

Directories:
* *Baileys Northern directory 1781;*
* Bilston 1770, 1780; 1781;
* Birmingham 1767-98 (13 directories);
* Boston 1789, 1796 & 1798;
* Brighton 1799 & 1800;
* Bristol 1775 & 1793;
* Dudley 1770, 1780 & 1781;
* Hampshire 1784;
* Leeds 1797, 1798 & 1800;
* Newcastle upon Tyne 1778-1824 (8 directories);
* London 1674-1783 (52 directories);
* St. Helena 1830;
* Sheffield 1774, 1787 & 1797;
* Walsall 1770, 1780 & 1781;
* Wolverhampton 1770, 1780 & 1781;
* *A musical directory for the year 1794/Joseph Doane.*
* 1487 book subscription lists;
* births marriages and deaths etc. from the *Gentleman's magazine,* 1731-50;
* membership lists of the Royal Society to 1815, and of the Literary & Philosophical Society, Newcastle, 1793-1815;
* biographical data from St. Helena
* apprenticeship lists from the Stationer's Company 1701-1800.

CD2 contents:

Directories:
* *Baileys British directory 1784* (4 vols.);
* Birmingham 1775-1801 (6 directories);
* Bristol 1785-99 (6 directories);
* Dover and Deal 1792;
* Edinburgh 1774, 1776;
* Glasgow 1783, 1787, 1789, 1791;
* Liverpool 1766 & 1774;
* London 1780-90 (23 directories);
* Manchester, 1772 & 1773;

- United States (Albany, Boston & Brooklyn) 1718-1830 (43 directories);
- 241 subscription lists, 1705-1833;
- births, deaths and marriages etc. from the *Gentleman's magazine,* 1751-1770;
- various learned society membership lists, *etc.*

CD3 contents:
Directories:
- Aberdeen 1824-30 (6 directories);
- Angus 1829 & 1830;
- Ayr 1830;
- Dundee 1782-1829 (6 directories);
- Edinburgh 1774-1830 (37 directories);
- Glasgow 1801-30 (28 directories);
- Greenock 1815, 1820, & 1828;
- Paisley 1810-1828 (6 directories);
- Renfrewshire 1829 & 1830;
- Aberystwyth 1816;
- Cardiff 1796, 1813 & 1829;
- Swansea 1802 & 1830;
- United States directories (Baltimore, Boston & Charleston) 1752-1829 (35 directories);
- London 1790;
- Cheltenham 1800;
- Gorleston 1828;
- Whitehaven 1762 (a manuscript local census);
- Scottish book subscription lists to 1800;
- Welsh book subscription lists to 1820;
- membership lists of the Society of Arts, 1772 & 1783-1800.

CD4 & CD5. Forthcoming; details to be announced.

The nineteenth-century short-title catalogue. 12 CD's (in progress). Personal research edition of series I & II (on 1 CD) £120.75 (inc. p&p & VAT). Listing of all British, British Empire and American publications 1801-1919 held in major British and American libraries, including much genealogical material. Series I includes the holdings of the British Library, the Bodleian Library, Cambridge University Library, Trinity College, Dublin, the National Library of Scotland, and the University of Newcastle upon Tyne for publications issued 1801-70. Series II records the holdings of the Library of Congress and Harvard University for the same period. For details of later series consult the publisher.

Adelaide Proformat
7 East Terrace, South Plympton,
South Australia 5038, Australia

Webpage: www.users.on.net/proformat/finder.html

A parish finder for England. $A41.80 + p&p. Lists parishes.

Ancestry.com

Mail Stop #B3-A, 360 West 4800 North, Provo, UT., 84604, U.S.A.
Email: psentz@myfamilyinc.com
Webpages: www.myfamily.com
www.ancestry.com

Biography and genealogy master index. $US39.95. Index to sources for biographical information on 1,400,000 people

Cambridge University alumni 1261-1900. $US29.95. Taken from Venn's *Alumni Cantabrigienses.*

The Great Migration begins: immigrants to New England 1620-1633. $US59.95. Details of 1,000+ migrants.

Irish vital records. Forthcoming. Will include Irish famine immigrants list, Irish flax growers list, *etc.*

Irish-Scots to America. Forthcoming. Includes various Scottish and Irish immigration records.

Various titles on emigrants to North America are under consideration.

Archive CD Books

51, St. Whites Road, Cinderford, Gloucestershire, GL14 3DF.
Phone: (01594) 829359
Fax: 0870 054 3701
Email: enquiries@archivecdbooks.com
Webpage: www.archivecdbooks.com

Prices

Please add £1.43 (UK) or £2.39 (overseas) for postage and packing. VAT may also be charged

General Interest

A topographical dictionary of England / S.Lewis. Originally published 1831 in 5 vols. 6 CDs. Ref.0100 £42.00. Includes a description of every place in England in 1831, with maps.

Cassell's Gazetteer of Great Britain & Ireland. Originally published 1898. Forthcoming.

Scroope extracts of wills 1630. Originally published 1934. Ref.0047. £8.50. Abstracts of wills in the Prerogative Court of Canterbury

Soame extracts of wills 1620. Originally published 1904. Ref. 0048. £8.50. Abstracts of wills in the Prerogative Court of Canterbury.

Oxford: Brasenose College register 1509-1909. Originally published Oxford Historical Society, 1909. Ref. 0172. £8.50.

How to write the history of a family / W.P.W. Phillimore. Originally published in 2 vols., 1887. Ref. 0087. £8.50. A classic text.

Bedfordshire

1830 Pigot's directory of Bedfordshire. Ref. 0030. £8.50. Also includes Northamptonshire, Huntingdonshire and Cambridgeshire.

Bedfordshire 1864 Post Office (Kelly's) directory. Ref. 0118. £8.50.

Bedfordshire 1898 Kelly's Directory. Ref. 0108. Forthcoming.

Berkshire

1830 Pigot's directories of Oxfordshire, Berkshire, Buckinghamshire. Ref. 0025. £8.50.

Archive CD Books (*continued*)
Berkshire 1869 Kelly's directory. Ref. 0117. £8.50.
Berkshire Pigot's directories 1830 and 1844. Ref. 0185. £8.50.
These 2 CDs (0117 & 0185) also available as a 2 CD set, ref. 0186, £12.00.

Buckinghamshire *See also* Berkshire
Buckinghamshire 1844 Pigot's directory. Ref.0222.
Forthcoming.
Buckinghamshire 1864. Kelly's directory. Ref. 0129. £8.50

Cambridgeshire *See also* Bedfordshire and Essex
1839 Pigot's directory: Cambridgeshire. Ref. 0063.
Forthcoming.
Cambridgeshire 1916: Kelly's directory. Ref. 0137.
Forthcoming.

Cheshire
Gawsworth, Cheshire: a parish history. Ref. 0074. £8.50.
Forthcoming.
Registers of Upton in Overchurch, 1600-1812. Originally
published by the Parish Register Society, 1900. Ref. 0095.
£8.50.
1850 Bagshaw directory, Cheshire. Ref.0121. 2 CD set. £14.00
The national roll of the Great War, 1914-18: Salford. Ref. 0182.
£8.50.

Cornwall *See also* Devon
1830 Pigot's directory of Cornwall. Ref.0028. £8.50. Includes
Devon on the same CD.
1844 Pigot's directory. Ref. 0224. £8.50. Forthcoming.
Cornwall parish registers: marriages / W.P.W.Phillimore (ed.)
26 vols. Originally published 1900-35. 9 CD set. Ref. 0122-S.
£63.00.
Each CD is also available separately, as follows:
• CD 1. Ref. 0122-1. £8.50. Contents: Vol.1. Advent 1675-1812;
Davidstow 1676-1812; Forrabury 1676-1812; Lanteglos by
Camelford 1558-1812; Lesnewth 1569-1812; Michaelstow 1539-
1812; Minster 1676-1812; Otterham 1687-1812; St.Breward
1558-1812; St.Clether 1640-1812; St.Juliot 1656-1812; St.Teath
1558-1812; Trevalga 1539-1812. Vol.2; Egloskerry 1574-1812;
Laneast 1680-1812; Lanivet 1608-1812; Phillack 1572-1812;
St.Mabyn 1562-1812; St.Tudy 1560-1812; Tintagel 1588-1812;
Tremaine 1674-1812. Vol.3; Gwithian 1560-1812; St.Buryan
1654-1812; St.Just in Penwith 1599-1812; St.Levan 1694-1812;
St.Sennen 1676-1812; Towednack 1676-1812.
• CD 2. Ref. 0122-2. £8.50. Contents: Vol.4. Blisland 1539-1812;
Cardynham 1675-1812; Endellion 1684-1812; Helland 1677-
1812; Lanhydrock 1559-1812; Sheviock 1570-1812; St.Merryn
1689-1812; St.Minver 1559-1812; Warleggan 1682-1812. Vol.5.
Ludgvan 1563-1812; Sancreed 1559-1812; St.Breage 1559-1812;
St.Germoe 1674-1812. Vol.6; Egloshayle 1600-1812; Padstow
1599-1812; St.Kew 1564-1812; St.Sampson (Golant) 1568-1812;
Warleggan 1547-1718; Withiel 1568-1812;
• CD 3. Ref. 0122-3. £8.50. Contents: Vol.7. Manaccan 1633-
1812; Mawnan 1553-1812; Mylor 1673-1812; Perranarworthal
1684-1812; St.Sithney 1654-1812; Stythians 1654-1812. Vol.8;
Fowey 1568-1812; Lostwithiel 1609-1812; Luxulyan 1594-1812;
St.Cleer 1678-1812; Tywardreath 1642-1812. Vol.9; Lelant

1679-1812; Paul 1595-1812; St.Hilary 1676-1812; Zennor 1617-1812;

- CD 4. Ref. 0122-4. £8.50. Contents: Vol.10. Lanlivery 1600-1812; Menheniot 1554-1812; St.Ewe 1560-1812; St.Stephen in Brannel 1681-1812; St.Winnow 1622-1812. Vol.11; Bodmin 1559-1812; Lezant 1539-1812; St.Gorran 1668-1812; St.Wenn 1678-1812. Vol.12; Gulval 1686-1741; Gwinear 1560-1812; Madron 1674-1812; Morvah (see Madron post 1722) 1617-1722;
- CD 5. Ref. 0122-5. £8.50. Contents: Vol.13. Budock 1653-1812; St.Colan 1665-1812; St.Gluvias 1599-1812. Vol.14; Lewannick 1675-1812; St.Columb Minor 1560-1812; St.Issey 1596-1812; St.Ives 1653-1812; St.Mawgan in Meneage 1563-1812. Vol.15; Constantine 1571-1812; Perranuthnoe 1589-1812; St.Martin in Meneage 1563-1812; Wendron 1560-1812;
- CD 6. Ref. 0122-6. £8.50. Contents: Vol. 16. Lanherne Convent RC 1710-1834; Little Petherick (St.Petrock Minor); Perranzabuloe 1619-1812; St.Columb Major 1781-1812; St.Crantock 1559-1812; St.Cubert 1608-1812; St.Ervan 1602-1812; St.Eval 1631-1812; St.Mawgan in Pydar 1608-1812; St.Newlyn in Pydar 1559-1812; St.Petrock Minor 1636-1812. Vol.17; Boyton 1568-1812; Linkinhorne 1576-1812; Morwinstow 1558-1812; Pillaton 1557-1812; Roche 1578-1812; South Petherwin 1656-1812; St.Mellion 1558-1812. Vol. 18; Crowan 1674-1812; St.Agnes 1596-1812; St.Allen 1611-1812; St.Breock 1561-1812.
- CD 7. Ref. 0122-7. £8.50. Contents: Vol. 19. Boyton II 1754-1812; Camborne 1538-1812; Redruth 1614-1812. Vol.20; Botus Fleming 1550-1812; Kilkhampton 1539-1812; Poughill 1537-1812; St.Anthony in Meneage 1726-1812; St.Enoder 1571-1812; St.Erme 1614-1812; St.Erth 1563-1812. Vol.21; Helston 1599-1812; Landrake 1583-1812; Landulph 1541-1812; St.Dennis 1610-1812; St.Erney 1555-1812; Stratton 1674-1812;
- CD 8. Ref. 0122-8. £8.50. Contents: Vol.22. Kea 1653-1812; Kenwyn 1559-1812; Tregony 1661-1812. Vol.23. Cornelly 1679-1812; Ladock 1686-1812; Launcells 1642-1812; Marhamchurch 1558-1812; Probus 1641-1812; St.Stephen by Launceston 1566-1812; St.Veryan 1676-1812. Vol.24. Launceston 1559-1812; St.Keverne 1608-1812.
- CD 9. Ref. 0122-9. £8.50. Contents: Vol.25. Grade 1708-1812; Gwennap 1660-1812; Jacobstow 1656-1812; Landewednack 1654-1812; Poundstock 1615-1812; Ruan Major 1683-1812; Ruan Minor 1667-1812; Treneglos 1694-1812; Warbstow 1695-1812; Week St.Mary 1602-1812. Vol.26. Creed (with Grampound) 1611-1837; Gerrans 1538-1837; Philleigh 1613-1837; Ruan Lanyhorne 1608-1837; St.Clement 1538-1837; St.Just in Roseland 1538-1812; St.Michael Penkivel 1577-1837. Devon vol.1. Werrington 1654-1812.

Cornwall parish register transcripts: Falmouth. Originally published by the Devon and Cornwall Record Society, 1914. Ref. 0124. £8.50. Baptisms and marriages 1597-1802.

Cumberland

Cumberland 1848 Pigot' directory. Ref. 0098. £8.50. Forthcoming.

Cumberland 1901 Bulmer's directory. Ref.0115. 2 CDs. £14.00. Forthcoming.

Archive CD Books (*continued*)

Derbyshire *See also* Nottinghamshire

Derbyshire 1831 Pigot's directory. Ref. 0132. £8.50.

Kelly's 1881 directory, Derbyshire. Ref.0044. £8.50.

Derbyshire parish registers: marriages / W.P.W.Phillimore (ed.) 15 vols. originally published 1895-1901. 5 CD set. Ref. 0052-S. £35.00.

Each CD is also available separately, as follows:

- CD 1. Ref. 0052-1. £8.50. Contents: Vol.1. Boulton 1756-1812; Breaston 1719-1810; Church Broughton 1538-1812; Dale Abbey 1667-1813; Hault Hucknall 1660-1812; Heath *alias* Lownd or Lund 1682-1812; Mackworth 1603-1812; Ockbrook 1631-1812; Risley 1720-1812; Sandiacre 1581-1812; Stanley 1754-1812; Stanton by Dale 1605-1812. Vol.2. Brailsford 1653-1812; Duffield 1598-1766. Vol.3. Duffield 1766-1812; Kirk Ireton 1572-1812; Mellor 1678-1775; Spondon 1658-1812.

- CD 2. Ref. 0052-2. £8.50. Contents: Vol.4. Derby St.Alkmunds 1538-1812; Foremark 1663-1812; Quarndon 1755-1812; Tickenhall 1628-1812. Vol. 5. Chaddesden 1718-1812; Morton 1575-1812; Norton 1559-1812; Derby St. Michaels, 1559-1812; West Hallam 1638-1812. Vol. 6. Alvaston 1614-1812; Chellaston 1570-1812; Derby St.Peters 1558-1812; Kirk Langley 1654-1812; Normanton by Derby 1769-1810; Osmaston by Derby 1743-1812; Willington 1698-1812.

- CD 3. Ref. 0052-3. £8.50. Contents: Vol. 7. Horsley 1558-1812; Ilkeston 1588-1812; Kirk Hallam 1700-1837; Matlock 1637-1812. Vol. 8. Alsop en le Dale 1701-1837; Aston upon Trent 1667-1812; Barrow on Trent & Twyford 1657-1812; Ilkeston 1785-1791; Melbourne 1653-1812; Parwich 1639-1837; Smisby 1720-1812; Stanton by Bridge 1664-1837; Swarkeston 1604-1837; Weston upon Trent 1565-1812. Vol. 9. Derby. All Saints 1558-1837.

- CD 4. Ref. 0052-4. £8.50. Contents: Vol. 10. Derby St. Werburgh 1558-1837. Vol. 11. Beauchief 1560-1837; Beighton 1653-1837; Dronfield 1696-1837. Vol.12. Buxton 1718-1837; Chapel-en-le-Frith 1621-1837; Fairfield 1756-1837; Repton 1578-1837.

- CD 5. Ref. 0052-5. £8.50. Contents: Vol.13. Breadsall 1573-1837; Elvaston 1651-1837; Kedleston 1600-1837; Morley 1540-1837; Sawley 1656-1837; Smalley 1624-1837; Wilne 1540-1837. Vol. 14. Denby 1577-1834; Elwall 1557-1837; Longford 1539-1837; Pentrich 1640-1837; Pentrich protestation roll 1641; Shirland 1695-1837; Stanley 1754-1837; South Wingfield 1585-1837; South Wingfield protestation 1641. Vol.15. Heanor 1558-1837.

Devon *See also* Cornwall

1844 Pigot's directory of Devon. Ref. 0223. £8.50.

Devon 1923 Kelly's directory. Ref.0175. 2 CD set. £14.00.

North Devon and North Cornwall Baddeley's guide (1908). Ref. 0071. £8.50.

Dorset

1830 Pigot's directory of Dorset. Ref. 0215. £8.50.

1844 Pigot's directory of Dorset. Ref. 0217. £8.50.

Dorset 1873 return of owners of land. Ref.0213-10. £8.50. Forthcoming.

Durham

Durham 1834 Pigot's directory. Ref. 0097. £8.50. Forthcoming.
Durham 1848 Pigot's directory. Ref. 0150. £8.50. Forthcoming.
1894 Whellan's history, topography & directory of the County of Durham. Ref. 0023. £11.00.

Essex

Essex 1848 White's directory. Ref. 00134. Forthcoming.
Handbook of Essex, Suffolk, Norfolk & Cambridgeshire. (1892). Ref. 0015. £8.50.
Parish registers of Moze, 1550-1678. Originally published 1899. Ref. 0229. £8.50.
Essex: a dictionary of the county / G.Worley. Originally published 1915. Ref. 0019. £8.50.

Gloucestershire

Pigot's 1830 Gloucestershire directory. Ref. 0024. £8.50. Includes Bristol & suburbs, and a Herefordshire directory (2 vols. on 1 CD).
Pigot's 1844 Gloucestershire directory. Ref. 0038. £8.50. Includes Bristol, with Herefordshire directory (2 vols. on 1 CD).
Kelly's 1879 Gloucestershire directory. Ref. 0037. £8.50.
Kelly's 1894 Gloucestershire directory. Ref. 0036. £8.50.
Kelly's 1894 Bristol directory. Ref. 0166. £8.50.
Bristol 1906 Kelly's directory. 2 CD set. Ref. 0167. £14.00.
Gloucestershire 1906 Kelly's directory. Ref. 0169. £8.50.
Gloucestershire 1923 Kelly's directory. Ref. 0145. £8.50.
The Forest of Dean, Gloucestershire / H.G.Nicholls. Originally published 1858. Ref. 0058. £8.50. Historical account.
Our parish: history of Mangotsfield & Downend / A.Emlyn Jones. Ref.0059. £8.50.
A calendar of wills proved in the Consistory Court of the Bishop of Gloucester, 1541-1650. Originally published in the British Record Society's *Index Library,* 1895. Ref. 0080. £8.50.
A calendar of wills proved in the Consistory Court of the Bishop of Gloucester 1660-1800. Originally published in the British Record Society's *Index Library,* 1907. Ref. 0099. £8.50.
Historical, monumental and genealogical collections relative to the County of Gloucester / Ralp Bigland. 4 CD set. Ref. 0190. £27.00. An enormous collection of inscriptions, many of which have now disappeared, made between 1750-1781.

Hampshire

1830 Pigot's directory of Hampshire and the Isle of Wight. Ref. 0216. £8.50.
1844 Pigot's directory of Hampshire and the Isle of Wight. Ref. 0218. £8.50. Forthcoming.
1859 White's directory, Hampshire and the Isle of Wight. Ref. 0021. £8.50.
Hampshire 1873 return of owners of land. Ref. 0213-30. £8.50. Forthcoming.
1911 Kelly's directory, Hampshire. 2 CD set. Ref. 0067. £14.00. Forthcoming.

Archive CD Books (*continued*)
Herefordshire *See also* Gloucestershire
1835 Pigot's directory of Herefordshire. Ref. 0038. £8.50.
Herefordshire 1895 Kelly's directory. Ref. 0144. £8.50.
1937 Kelly's directory of Herefordshire. Ref. 0084. £8.50.

Hertfordshire
Hertfordshire little guide, 1903. Ref. 0170. £8.50. Tourist guide.

Huntingdonshire *See also* Bedfordshire

Isle of Man
Isle of Man 1825 Pigot' directory. Ref. 0209. £8.50.

Kent
Kent 1840 Pigot' directory. Ref. 0105. £8.50.

Lancashire
Manchester & Salford 1788 Lewis's directory. Ref. 0160. £8.50.
Lancashire 1824 Bain's directory. 2 CD set. Ref. 0107. £14.00.

Leicestershire *See also* Nottinghamshire
Leicestershire & Rutland 1841 Pigot's directory. Ref. 0133.
   £8.50.
Return of owners of land 1873: Leicestershire and Rutland.
   Ref. 0213-19. £8.50. Forthcoming.
White's directory, Leicestershire & Rutland 1877. 2 CD set.
   £14.00.
Kelly's 1881 directory, Leicestershire & Rutland, 1881. Ref.
   0046. £8.50. Forthcoming.
Leicestershire 1928 Kelly's directory. 2 CD set. Ref. 0173. £14.00.
Leicestershire parish registers: marriages / W.P.W.Phillimore
   (ed.) 12 vols. originally published 1908-14. 4 CD set. Ref.
   FWCO51. Entire set forthcoming. CD's currently available:
- CD 1. Ref. 0051-1. Contents: Vol. 1. Bottesford 1563-1812;
   Muston 1561-1812; Twyford cum Thorpe Satchville 1561-1812;
   Coston 1561-1812; Scraptoft 1539-1812; Sibson 1569-1812;
   Congerston 1756-1812; Ratby 1695-1812; Gaddesby 1569-1812.
   Vol.2. Ab Kettleby cum Holwell, 1580-1812; Scalford 1558-
   1812; Evington 1601-1837; Rotherby 1561-1812; Hoby 1562-
   1812; Frisby-on-the-Wreak 1569-1837; Ragdale 1688-1837;
   Brooksby 1767-1812; Thrussington 1660-1812; Barkby 1586-
   1812; Somerby 1601-1812; Kirby Bellars 1713-1837. Vol. 6.
   Ashby Folville 1584-1837; South Croxton 1662-1837;
   Hungerton 1614-1837; Beeby 1538-1837; Queniborough 1562-
   1837; Eastwell 1588-1837; Wartnaby 1633-1838; Grimston
   1635-1837; Cossington 1754-1837; Ratcliffe on the Wreak
   1698-1837; Seagrave 1682-1837; Syston 1663-1837.
- CD 2. Ref. FWCO51-2. £8.50. Contents: Vol.8. Owston cum
   Newbold Saucey, 1701-1837; Withcote 1681-1837; Wymeswold
   1560-1837; Sileby 1568-1837; Rearsby 1653-1837; Prestwold
   1560-1837; Hoton 1653-1837. Vol.9. Walton on the Wolds
   1568-1837; Quorndon 1576-1837; Woodhouse 1623-1837;
   Wanlip 1563-1837; Swithland 1624-1837; Humberstone 1559-
   1837; Vol.11. Goadby Marwood 1657-1837; Long Clawson
   1558-1837; Old Dalby 1725-1837; Nether Broughton 1577-1837;
   Saxelbye (with Sholeby) 1555-1837; Ashfordby 1564-1837;
   Thorpe Arnold (with Brentingby) 1558-1840; Wyfordby
   1558-1837; Saxby 1680-1837; Stapleford 1655-1837.

Lincolnshire *See also* Nottinghamshire

Lincolnshire 1818 poll book. Ref. 0114. £8.50.

Pigot's directory of Lincolnshire 1835. Ref. 0090. £8.50.

Pigot's directory of Lincolnshire 1841. Ref. 0011. £8.50.

Return of owners of land 1873: Lincolnshire. Ref. 0213-20. £8.50. Forthcoming.

Kelly's 1876 directory of Lincolnshire. 2 CD set. Ref. 0091. £14.00.

Lincolnshire 1913 Kelly's directory. 2 CD set. Ref. 0120. £14.00.

London

London marriage licences 1521-1869. Originally published 1887. Ref. 0068. £11.00. Includes names from throughout the country.

London 1848 Post Office (Kelly's) directory. 2 CD set. Ref. 0109. £14.00.

Middlesex

Parish registers, Middlesex: Chelsea St. Luke's burials 1559-1860. 2 CD set. Ref. 0180. £14.00. From the original registers.

Parish registers, Middlesex: Chelsea St. Luke's baptisms 1559-1860. 2 CD set. Ref. 0181. £14.00. From the original registers.

Parish registers, Middlesex: Chelsea St. Luke's marriages. Forthcoming.

Monmouthshire *See also* Wales

1830 & 1844 Pigot's directory, Monmouthshire. Ref. 0225. £8.50.

Parish registers of Grosmont, 1589-1812. Originally published 1926. Ref. 0081. £8.50.

Norfolk *See also* Essex

1830 Pigot's directory of Norfolk. Ref. 0029. £8.50. Includes directory of Suffolk.

Norfolk 1916 Kelly's directory. 2 CD set. Ref. 0135. £14.50. Forthcoming.

Norfolk 1933 Kelly's directory. 2 CD set. Ref. 0165. £14.50. Forthcoming.

Northamptonshire *See also* Bedfordshire

Northamptonshire parish registers: marriages / W.P.W.Phillimore (ed.) Originally published 1908- . Ref. 0086-1. £8.50. Contents: Castor 1538-1812; Croughton 1663-1812; Dodford 1581-1812; Everdon 1558-1837; Farthingstone 1538-1812; Faxton 1570-1837; Glinton 1567-1812; Harpole 1538-1812; Heyford 1558-1837; Lamport 1587-1837; Northampton St. Peter's 1578-1812; Northborough 1538-1812; Peakirk 1617-1812; Stoke Bruerne 1561-1837; Stowe Nine Churches 1560-1837; Weston by Welland and Sutton Bassett 1570-1812.

Northumberland

Northumberland 1829 and 1834 Pigot's directories. Ref. 0101SE. £8.50. Forthcoming. This CD will eventually be replaced by separate CDs for each directory.

Archive CD Books (*continued*)

1855 Whellan's directory Northumberland. 2 CD set. Ref. 0062. £14.00.

Northumberland 1879 Post Office directory (Kelly's). Ref. 0110. £8.50.

Nottinghamshire

1832 White's Nottinghamshire directory. Ref. 0008. £8.50.

White's 1853 directory of Nottingham. Ref. 0057. £8.50. Forthcoming.

1854 Nottingham directory with suburbs / C.N.Wright. Ref. 0032. £8.50.

1869 Morris & Co. directory of Nottinghamshire, with Grantham, Chesterfield and Gainsborough. Ref. 0033. £8.50.

1871 return of owners of land, Nottinghamshire. Ref. 0213-26. £8.50.

Nottingham & district 1877 Morris & Co. directory. Ref. 0142. £8.50.

1881 Kelly's directory of Nottinghamshire. Ref. 0045. £8.50. Forthcoming.

1883 Nottingham, S.Notts., & 24 miles around Nottingham Wright's directory. 2 CD set. Ref. 0141. £14.00.

Wright's directory 1888/9: twelve miles around Nottingham. Ref. 0010. £8.50. Includes Ilkeston and other parts of Derbyshire and Leicestershire.

Nottinghamshire 1891 Kelly's directory. Ref. 0126. £8.50.

Nottinghamshire 1900 Kelly's directory. 2 CD set. Ref. 0139. £14.00.

1915 directory of Nottingham and neighbourhood / C.N.Wright. 2 CD set. Ref. 0035. £14.00 Forthcoming.

Nottinghamshire 1922 Kelly's directory. 2 CD set. £14.00

The Nottingham date book, 850-1884. Originally published 1884.

Royal charters of the Borough of Nottingham 1155-1712. Originally published 1890. Ref. 0003. £8.50.

Records of the Borough of Nottingham. 9 CD's. Ref. 0005. Forthcoming. Vol.1. (0005-1) 1155-1399 now available. £8.50.

Old Nottingham: streets and people. Ref. 0006. £8.50.

Annals of Nottinghamshire / Bailey. Originally published in 4 vols., 1853.

Return of owners of land 1873: Nottinghamshire. Ref. 0213-26. £8.50.

Nottinghamshire old books, vol.1. Ref. 0016. £8.50. Forthcoming. Compendium of 7 historical studies of the county.

Newark. Ref. 0017. Forthcoming. Includes:
- *Annals of Newark / Cornelius Brown.*
- *A guide to Newark / Thomas Blagg.*

Magna Britannia antiqua & nova for Nottinghamshire. Originally published 1738. Ref. 0020. £8.50.

Deerings history of Nottingham / Charles Deering. Originally published 1751. Ref. 0049. Forthcoming.

Pipe rolls of Nottingham & Derby. Ref.0054. £8.50. Forthcoming.

The journal and diary of John Savidge. (Methodist city missionary) January 1896-June 1898. Ref. 0056. £8.50. From the original.

Notes about Notts / Cornelius Brown. Originally published 1874. Ref. 0064. £8.50. Forthcoming.

Nottingham Council House opening 1929. Ref. 0070. £8.50.

History of the parish and priory of Lenton. Ref. 0076. £8.50.

Nottinghamshire county records, 17th century. Ref. 0078. £8.50. Forthcoming.

The book of Nottingham,. with *Lists of Nottingham burgesses enrolled 1702-3 & 1760-1800.* Ref. 0164. £8.50. The *Book . . .* originally published 1926.

Nottinghamshire parish registers: marriages / W.P.W.Phillimore (ed.) Ref. 0050-1. £8.50. Includes the registers of the Nottingham parishes of St.Mary, St.Peter, and St.Nicholas. More vols. from this series forthcoming.

Oxfordshire *See also* Berkshire

1844 Pigot's directory, Oxfordshire. Ref. 0221. £8.50. Forthcoming.

1864 Oxfordshire Kelly's directory. Ref. 0112. £8.50. Forthcoming.

1869 Oxfordshire Kelly's directory. Ref. 0138. £8.50.

Oxford: Brasenose College register 1509-1909. Originally published 1909 Ref. 0172. £8.50.

Rutland *See also* Leicestershire

1928 Kelly's directory, Rutland. Ref. 0174. £8.50. Forthcoming.

Shropshire

1844 Shropshire Pigot's directory. Ref. 0096. £8.50. Forthcoming.

1895 Shropshire Kelly's directory. Ref. 0143. £8.50. Forthcoming.

1934 Kelly's directory of Shropshire. Ref. 0085. £8.50. Forthcoming.

Somerset

1825 Pigot's directory of Somerset. Ref. 0146. £8.50. Forthcoming.

1830 Pigot's directory of Somerset. Ref. 0026. £8.50. Includes Wiltshire directory.

1844 Pigot's directory of Somerset. Ref. 0219. £8.50.

Staffordshire

1835 Pigot's directory, Staffordshire. Ref. 0094. £8.50.

Suffolk (See also) Norfolk

Suffolk hearth tax returns 1674. Originally published 1905. Ref. 0228. £8.50.

1825 Pigot's directory of Suffolk. Ref. 0147. £8.50.

1830 Pigot's directory of Suffolk. Ref. 0029. £8.50.

1839 Pigot's directory of Suffolk. Ref. 0131. £8.50.

1916 Kelly's directory of Suffolk. Ref. 0136. £14.00

Sussex

Sussex 1840 Pigot's directory. Ref. 0106. £8.50.

Sussex 1851 Kelly's directory. Ref. 0116. £8.50.

Sussex 1899 Kelly's directory. 2 CD set. Ref. 0127. £14.00

Sussex 1911 Kelly's directory. 2 CD set. Ref. 0128. £14.00

The parish registers of Hove and Preston 1538-1812 / Ernest Salmon (ed.) Ref. 0192. £8.50.

Archive CD Books (*continued*)

Warwickshire

Warwickshire 1835 Pigot's directory. Ref. 0089. £8.50.

1850 White's directory of Warwickshire. 2 CD set. Ref. 0018.
£14.00

Westmorland

1834 Westmorland Pigot's directory. Ref. 0151. £8.50.
Forthcoming.

Wiltshire *See also* Somerset

1825 Pigot's directory of Wiltshire. Ref. 0148. £8.50.

1844 Pigot's directory of Wiltshire. Ref. 0220. £8.50.

Wiltshire 1895 Kelly's directory. Ref. 0119. £8.50.

Highway's & byways in Wiltshire / Hutton. Originally
published 1914. Ref. 0077. £8.50.

Worcestershire

Worcestershire 1835 Pigot's directory. Ref. 0088. £8.50.
Forthcoming.

Bentley's 1840/41 directory of Worcestershire. Ref. 0034.
£11.00.

A century of progress 1831-1931: Cadbury Bournville. Ref.
0061. £8.50.

Bournville collection. Ref. 0066. £8.50. 5 old books about
Cadbury & Bourneville

Worcestershire magna Britannia. Originally printed 1721. Ref.
0140. £8.50.

Yorkshire

1837 White's directory of Yorkshire West Riding. Ref. 0125.
£8.50. Forthcoming.

Ossett burgess roll 1905-6 & 1912-14. Ref. 0014. £8.50.

Through guides: Yorkshire (Baddeley). Originally published
1907. £8.50. Forthcoming. Tourist guide.

Guide to Sheffield. Ref. 0092. £8.50. Forthcoming.

Reminiscences of old Sheffield. Originally published 1876.
Ref. 0093. £8.50. Forthcoming.

Sheffield handbook and guide. Ref. 0184. £8.50. Forthcoming.

The national roll of the Great War: Leeds. Ref. 0163. £8.50.
Forthcoming.

Wales

1830 Pigot's directory of South Wales. Ref. 0031. £8.50.
Includes directory of Monmouthshire.

1844 Pigot's directory, North Wales. Ref. 0227. £8.50.
Forthcoming.

1844 Pigot's directory, South Wales. Ref. 0226. £8.50.
Forthcoming.

Return of owners of land 1873: Wales. 3 CD set. 0214-S.
£21.00. Forthcoming. Individual CD's may also be available
separately.

Breconshire

History of Brecknockshire / Theophilus Jones. Originally
published in 4 vols., 1909. Ref. 0239. 2 or 3 CD set.
Forthcoming.

Caernarvonshire

Parish registers of Conway 1541-1793. Ref. 0082. £8.50.

Scotland

Scotland: 1825/6 combined Pigot's directory. 5 CD set. Ref. 0206. £35.00. Forthcoming. Individual CD's also available separately as follows:

- *1825/6 Pigot's directories: Central East Scotland.* Ref. 0201. £8.50. Forthcoming. Includes directory for Edinburgh, Fife, Haddington and Linlithgow.
- *1825/6 Pigot's directories: Southern Highlands area.* Ref. 0202. £8.50. Forthcoming. Includes directories for Argyll, Bute, Perth, Forfar or Angus, and Stirling.
- *1825/6 Pigot's directories: Highlands area.* Ref. 0203. £8.50. Forthcoming. Includes directories for Aberdeen, Banff, Caithness, Elgin or Morayshire, Inverness, Kincardineshire or Mearns, Nairn, Orkneys, Ross & Cromarty, and Sutherland.
- *1825/6 Pigot's directories: Central Scotland.* Ref. 0204. £8.50. Forthcoming. Includes directories for Ayr, Clackmannan, Dumbarton, Lanark, and Renfrew.
- *1825/6 Pigot's directories: South Scotland.* Ref. 0205. £8.50. Forthcoming. Includes directories for Berwick, Dumfries, Kirkcudbright, Peebles, Roxburgh, Selkirk and Wigtown; also 'alphabetical reference to the nobility, gentry and clergy in all the cities and towns, etc., of Scotland' (except Edinburgh).

Aberdeen 1925 Post Office directory. Ref. 0234. Forthcoming.

Kilbarchan: a parish history. Ref. 0022. £8.50.

Topographical dictionary of Scotland / S Lewis. Originally published 1831 in 2 vols. Ref. 0130. £14.00. Forthcoming.

Scotland: Imperial gazetteer. Originally published in 2 vols., 1868. Ref. 0231. Forthcoming.

Scotland: Ordnance gazetteer. Originally published 1881. Ref.0162. £8.50. Forthcoming.

The Shire of Renfrew / George Crawfurd & George Robertson. Originally published in 2 vols., 1718-1818. Ref. 0161. £8.50.

Curiosities of Glasgow citizenship. Originally published 1881. Ref. 0162. £8.50. Forthcoming.

The social life of Scotland in the 18th century. Ref. 0230. Forthcoming.

Ireland

Ireland: the Treble almanack 1818. Ref. 0152. £8.50. Forthcoming.

Ireland: the Treble almanack 1822. Ref. 0153. £8.50. Forthcoming.

Ireland: the Treble almanack 1829. Ref. 0154. £8.50. Forthcoming.

Ireland: the Dublin almanack & general register of Ireland 1836. Ref. 0155. £8.50.

Forthcoming.

Ireland: Thorn's Irish almanack & official directory, 1877. Ref. 0156. Forthcoming.

Ireland: Thorn's Irish almanack & official directory 1879. Ref. 0157. Forthcoming.

Ireland: Thorn's Irish almanack & official directory 1880. Ref. 0158. Forthcoming.

Back to Roots Family History Service

16 Arrowsmith Drive, Stonehouse, Gloucestershire, GL10 2QR.
Agents for Family History Indexes, which see.

Gordon Beavington

560 Hemlock Road, Kelowna, B.C., VIX 5G4, Canada.
Email: gordon@mycensuses.com
Webpage: www.mycensuses.com

Gloucestershire and Southern Warwickshire 1851+. CD3.
   £12.00; $A30.00; $US20.00; $NZ35.00; $C22.80. 1851 and
   later censuses; 552,000 records in all.
Bristol and Bedminster 1851 census. CD4. £8.00; $A20.00;
   $US15.00; $NZ25.00; $16.60. Includes Shirehampton,
   Henbury, Westbury on Trym, Filton, Stoke Gifford,
   Winterbourne and Stapleton.
Somerset 1851 census. CD7. £18.00. Forthcoming.

Bookmarks Family History Software

39, Barnfield Crescent, Wellington, Telford, TF1 2EU.
Webpage: members.tripod.co.uk/familyhistory2/

Internet Bookmarks. £6.00 + p&p. Directory to 600 websites.

June Borderick

65 Greengate Lane, Birstall, Leicester LE4 3JG.
Email: june.borderick@ntlworld.com.

Phillimore Leicestershire marriages. £20.00. Contents:
   Ab-Kettleby-cum-Holwell, 1580-1812; Asfordby, 1564-1837;
   Ashford Folville, 1604-1837; Ashby Parva, 1589-1837;
   Aylestone with Glen Parva and Lubbesthorpe, 1561-1837;
   Barkby, 1586-1812; Barkston, 1569-1837; Barrow-on-Soar,
   1563-1837; Beeby, 1538-1837; Belgrave, 1653-1837; Birstall,
   1574-1837; Bitteswell, 1558-1837; Blaby, 1568-1837; Bottesford,
   1563-1812; Branston, 1591-1839; Braunston, 1561-1837;
   Brooksby, 1767-1812; Burrough, 1612-1837; Burton Lazars,
   1762-1778, Catthorpe, 1573-1837; Congerston, 1756-1812,
   Cossington, 1754-1837, Coston, 1561-1812; Croxton Kerrial,
   1558-1837; Eastwell, 1588-1837; Eaton, 1724-1837; Evington,
   1601-1837; Freeby, 1601-1775; Frisby on the Wreak, 1659-
   1837; Frolesworth, 1538-1837; Gaddesby, 1569-1812;
   Gilmorton, 1611-1837; Glenfield, 1604-1837; Goadby
   Marwood, 1657-1837; Great Dalby, 1581-1812; Grimston, 1635-
   1837; Harby, 1700-1837; Harston, 1707-1837; Hoby, 1562-1812;
   Hose, 1688-1837; Hoton, 1653-1837; Houghton-on-the-Hill,
   1584-1837; Humberstone, 1559-1837; Hungerton (which
   includes Baggrave, Quenby, and Ingersby) 1614-1837;
   Keyham, 1568-1837; Kirby Bellars, 1712-1837; Kirby Muxloe,
   1619-1837 Knighton, 1672-1837; Knipton, 1562-1837; Leire,
   1559-1837; Little Dalby, 1559-1812; Long Clawson, 1558-1837;
   Lowesby with Cold Newton, 1658-1837; Melton Mowbray,
   (includes Burton Lazars, Freeby, Sysonby, Welby and Eye-
   Kettleby) 1546-1812; Mountsorrel (North End), 1677-1837;
   Muston, 1561-1812; Nether Broughton, 1577-1837; Old Dalby,
   1725-1837; Owston-cum-Newbold Saucey, 1701-1837;

Pickwell, 1570-1841; Plungar, 1695-1837; Prestwold (including Burton-on-the-Wolds, and Cotes), 1560-1837; Queniborough, 1562-1837; Quorndon, 1576-1837; Ragdale, 1668-1837; Ratby, 1695-1812; Ratcliffe-on-the-Wreak, 1698-1837; Rearsby, 1653-1837; Redmile, 1653-1837; Rotherby, 1561-1812; Rothley, 1562-1837; Saxby, 1680-1837; Scalford, 1558-1812; Scraptoft, 1539-1812; Seagrave, 1682-1837; Sharnford, 1595-1837; Sibson, 1569-1812; Sileby, 1568-1837; Somerby, 1601-1812; South Croxton, 1662-1837; Stapleford, 1655-1837; Stathern, 1567-1837; Stoughton, 1537-1837; Swithland, 1624-1837; Syston, 1562-1837; Thorpe Arnold with Brentingby, 1558-1840; Thrussington, 1660-1812; Thurcaston-cum-Cropston, 1561-1837; Thurmaston, 1719-1837; Thurnby-cum-Bushby, 1564-1837; Tilton-on-the-Hill, 1631-1837; Twyford-cum-Thorpe Satchville, 1562-1812; Walton-on-the-Wolds, 1568-1837; Wanlip, 1563-1837; Wartnaby, 1633-1838; Wigston Magna, 1567-1837; Withcote, 1681-1837; Woodhouse, 1623-1837; Wyfordby, 1558-1837; Wykeham-cum-Caldwell or Caudwell, 1663-1837, Wymeswold, 1560-1837.

Dr.B.N.Bowden
Carwhin, West Park, Leslie, Fife, Scotland KY6 3EY.

System Requirements: Word 97

A Bowden family: its history and genealogy. £12.00. Also available in book format.

Buckinghamshire Genealogical Society
Varneys, Rudds Lane, Haddenham, Bucks., HP17 8JP.
MACH 1891 census for Buckinghamshire. Version 2.1. £15.00 + p&p £1.00 (UK) or £1.50 (overseas)

Carmarthenshire Family History Society
P.O.Box 41, Llanelli, SA15 9YP.
Email: Bookpurchase@WalesGenealogy.co.uk
Webpage: www.carmarthenshirefhs.btinternet.co.uk

Carmarthenshire 1851 census index, part 1. £17.50.
Carmarthenshire marriages 1754-1812. £12.00. Index of 27,500+ marriages; includes a few marriages pre-1754.
Dyfed marriages 1812-1837. £15.00 Index of 45,000 marriages in Cardiganshire, Carmarthenshire & Pembrokeshire.
Marriage bonds & fiats of West Wales & Gower 1612-1800. £10.00. Abstract & index.
Llanelly. St. Elli parish church registers. £10.00. Marriages 1687-1837; baptisms 1687-1832; burials 1693-1847. Index.
Cardiganshire marriages 1813-1837. £10.00
Carmarthenshire marriages 1813-1837. £10.00
Pembrokeshire marriages 1813-1837. £10.00
Genealogies of the Carmarthenshire sheriffs 1593-1913 / James Buckley. Originally published in 2 vols, 1910-13.
A history of Carmarthenshire / Sir John E. Lloyd. Originally published in 2 vols, 1935. £17.50.
Carmarthenshire anthology vol.1. £10.00. Contents:
  • Carmarthen town inns 1822;
  • Carmarthen town directory 1793;

Carmarthenshire Family History Society (*continued*)
- Carmarthenshire map of parishes & commencement dates of parish registers;
- Carmarthenshire map of ancient hundreds;
- Carmarthenshire parishes;
- Carmarthenshire church & nonconformist chapel records & where they can be found;
- Carmarthenshire marriages 1813-1837;
- Carmarthenshire wills index 1564-1858;
- Carmarthen town census names index 1851;
- Vicars of Eglwys Cymmin;
- Kidwelly baillifs 1618-1843;
- Kidwelly inns & publicans 1837;
- Kidwelly town directory 1793;
- Llanelly town census names index 1851;
- Lords of the manor of Eglwys Cymmin 1207-1943;
- Scurlock's of Carmarthenshire;
- The parish of St.Ishmael's and its ancient church.

Pembrokeshire anthology volume 1. £10.00. Contents:
- Barlows of Slebech;
- Camrose monumental inscriptions;
- Cilgerran Weir;
- Early wills of Pembrokeshire;
- Evan Lloyd of Hendre, Pembs;
- Haverford records;
- Lord Lieutenants of Pembrokeshire & Haverfordwest;
- Manor of Castellan;
- Mayors of Pembrokeshire;
- Musgrave of Llanina;
- Pembrokeshire directory 1793;
- Pembrokeshire hearths 1670;
- Pembrokeshire lay subsidies;
- Pembrokeshire marriages 1813-1837;
- Pembrokeshire parishes;
- Pembrokeshire sheriffs;
- Pictons of Poyston;
- Rudbaxton monumental inscriptions;
- Rudbaxton: notes on the parish;
- Saunders of Pentre, Tymawr & Glynrhydw;
- Sir John Stepney of Prendergast;
- Stepneys of Prendergast;
- Thomas Bowen of Trefloyn;
- Tuckers of Sealyham;
- Walter of Roch Castle;
- Wogans of Pembrokeshire.

Old Llanelli / John Innes. Originally published 1903. £10.00

Antiquities of Laugharne, Pendine, and their neighbourhoods / Mary Curtis. Originally published 1880. £10.00

Llandilo past & present / W. Samuell. Originally published 1868. £10.00

History of Caio / Fred Price. £10.00

Carmarthen and its neighbourhood / William Spurrell. Originally published 1879. £10.00

Llannelly directory 1897. £10.00

St.Illtyd's church, Pembrey: its history and architecture / Edward Roberts & H.A.Pertwee. Originally published 1898.

Cassell's gazetteer of Great Britain & Ireland. Originally published 1893-8. £27.50

Handbook of the origins of Place names of Wales & Monmouthshire / Thomas Morgan. Originally published 1887. £15.00

West Wales historical records volume 1-14. £19.95. Complete run of an important historical journal with many articles of genealogical interest. See web-page for a complete list of articles.

Topographical dictionary of Wales / Samuel Lewis. 1842 edition. £15.00.

Cary's new map of England and Wales with part of Scotland 1794. £19.95.

Chadwyck-Healey

The Quorum, Barnwell Road, Cambridge CB5 8SW.
Phone: 01223 271254
Webpage: www.chadwyck.co.uk

British Library general catalogue of printed books to 1995 on CD-Rom. Price on application.
British national bibliography on CD-Rom. Price on application.
Palmers index to the Times 1790-1905. Price on application.
The official index to the Times 1906-1980. Price on application.

Church of Jesus Christ of Latter Day Saints

The Distribution Centre, 399 Garretts Green Lane, Birmingham, B33 OUH.
Webpage: www.familysearch.org

Family History Library catalogue. Item #50081. £5.95 (inc p&p). Listing of 2,500,000 microforms & 300,000 books in the library.

British 1881 census. Item #50169. 25 discs. £29.95 (inc p&p). Please inquire for particular regions.

Pedigree discs 1-5 complete with index disc. Item #50250. £14.95 (inc p&p). Ditto, 6-10 (50251), 11-15 (50252), and 16-20 (50253), all £14.95 each. Tens of thousands of lineage e-linked pedigrees, including notes and sources.

1851 census for Devon, Norfolk and Warwick. Item #50096. £5.95 (inc p&p).

British Isles Vital Records. 6 CDs. Item #50028. £14.95 (inc p&p). Index of parish registers, 1538-1888.

Francis Coakley

Senior Lecturer, Rm 18BB02, Dept.of Electrical Engineering, University of Surrey, Guildford GU2 7XH.
Phone: (0) 14837 879129
Email: f.coakley@eim.surrey.ac.uk
Webpage: www.ee.surrey.ac.uk/Contrib/manx/index.htm

A Manx note book: an electronic compendium of matters past and present connected with the Isle of Man. £8.50. CD version of the extensive web-page, with additional materials, and including the text of c.100 Manx monographs, including a number of directories.

Cornish Forefathers Society

c/o Mrs. Pam Drake, Credvill, Quakers Road, Perranwell,
Truro, Cornwall TR3 7PJ.
Email: Pam@cornish-forefathers.com
Webpage: www.cornish-forefathers.com

Note

All the following publications are in ASCII text on floppy
disk. Many more parishes are forthcoming. It is hoped to issue
them on CD in the future.

Breage baptisms 1724-1839. 3½" floppy disk. £7.50.
Gerrans baptisms 1716-1845. 3½" floppy disk. £3.50.
Lanivet baptisms 1700-1840. 3½" floppy disk. £3.50.
Mevagissey baptisms 1720-1840. 3½" floppy disk. £5.00.
Rame by Plymouth baptisms 1714-1841. 3½" floppy disk. £4.00.
St.Dominick baptisms 1737-1841. 3½" floppy disk. £2.00.
St.Germans baptisms 1720-1840. 3½" floppy disk. £4.50.
St.Ives baptisms 1720-1840. 3½" floppy disk. £6.50.
St.Neot baptisms 1710-1840. 3½" floppy disk £4.00.

Cornwall Business Systems

CBS House, Albany Road, Redruth, Cornwall. TR15 2HY.
Phone: (01209) 217616
Email: Laurence@CornishRoots.co.uk
Webpage: www.cornishroots.co.uk

Prices

Prices include p&p world-wide.

Cornish roots! £41. Contents: 1851 census (part); gazetteer;
emigrants; maps; Cornish places; famous people; family
names; place names; musical slideshows.
Cornwall multi-media: movies, music and magic! £6.00.
Contents: sights; attractions; history; Cornish family names;
Cornish place-names; maps; musical slide-show.
The Cornish Gedcom file. £5.00 (or free if you submit a
Gedcom file). Contents: over 32,000 records of individuals
and their families.
Cornish characters and strange events / S.Baring-Gould. £6.00.
Originally published in 1909.
*Visitations of Cornwall: the heralds visitations of 1530, 1573 &
1620 / J.L. Vivian.* £32.00. Originally published 1887.
1851 census for Cornwall. £30.00. Registration districts
included. Bodmin; Launceston; Liskeard; St.Austell,
St.Columb.
25,000 records of Cornish emigrants to America. £20.00
Gazetteer of Cornwall, 1884 on CD / R.Symons. £20.00.
Originally published 1884.
Kelly's directory for Cornwall, 1883 on CD. £32.00
Venning's postal directory of East Cornwall 1901. £10.00.
Coulson's postal directory of Penzance 1864. £8.00.
Directory of Redruth 1866 on CD. £12.00

Cornwall Legacy
See Shelkay

Direct Resources
33A Ruskin Avenue, Wakefield, WF1 2BG.
Phone: (07974) 672648
Emmail: enquiries@direct-resources.uk.com
Webpage: www.direct-resources.uk.com

System Requirements
Ideally a good spreadsheet is needed.

Prices
£15.00 + p&p per CD.

Bedfordshire 1847. Includes Ampthill, Bedford, Biggleswade, Dunstable, Leighton Buzzard, Luton, Woburn. Extracts from *Kelly's Post Office 1847 Bedfordshire directory.*

Berkshire 1847. Includes Abingdon, Farringdon, Hungerford, Newbury, Reading, Wantage, Wokingham. Extracts from *Post Office Berkshire 1855 directory.*

Buckinghamshire 1847. Includes Aylesbury, Buckingham, Chesham, Marlow, Newport Pagnell, Olney, High Wycombe. Extracts from *Kelly's Post Office 1847 Buckinghamshire directory.*

Cambridgeshire 1846. Includes Cambridge, Chatteris, Ely, Littleport, March, Newmarket, Soham, Upwell, Whittlesey, Wisbeach. Extracts from *Kelly's Cambridge Post Office 1846 directory.*

Cheshire 1848. Includes Altrincham, Ashton under Lyne, Cheadle, Chester, Congleton, Ellesmere Port, Knutsford, Macclesfield, Middlewich, Northwich, Runcorn, Stockport. Extracts from *Slater's Cheshire directory 1848.*

Cornwall 1850. Includes Bodmin, Camborne, Falmouth, Helston, Launceston, Liskeard, Penzance, Redruth, Truro. Extracts from *Williams' directory of Cornwall 1850.*

Cumberland 1847. Includes Alston, Bowness, Carlisle 1790, 1829, 1847, Cockermouth, Hawkeshead, Keswick, Maryport, Penrith, Whitehaven, Wigton, Workington. Extracts from: *Mannix & Whellan's Cumberland directory, 1847, Slater's Lancashire directory, 1848, & Mannix & Whellan's Durham directory, 1847.*

Derbyshire 1846. Includes Alfreton, Ashbourn, Ashover, Bakewell, Belper, Bolsover, Brampton, Burton upon Trent, Buxton, Chapel en le Frith, Chesterfield, Crich, Cromford, Darley, Derby, Duffield, Eckington, Glossop, Heanor, Ilkeston, Matlock, Melbourne, Mosborough, New Mills, Norton, Repton, Ripley, Staveley, Tideswell, Wirksworth. Extracts from *Bagshaw's Derbyshire directory 1846.*

Devon 1850. Includes Axminster, Barnstaple, Bideford, Crediton, Exeter, Exmouth, Plymouth, Tavistock, Tiverton, Great Torrington. Extracts from *White's Devon directory 1850.*

Dorset 1848. Includes Blandford, Bridport, Dorchester, Poole, Shaftesbury, Sherborne, Wareham, Weymouth, Wimborne. Extracts from *Kelly's Post Office 1848 Dorset directory.*

Direct Resources (*continued*)

Essex 1848. Includes Barking, Braintree, Brentwood, Chelmsford, Coggleshall, Colchester, Epping, Great Dunmow, Halstead, Harwich, Ilford, Manningtree, Maldon, Romford, Saffron Walden, Walthamstow, Waltham Abbey, Westham / Stratford, Witham. Extracts from *White's 1848 Essex directory,* & *Kelly's Essex Post Office directory 1846.*

Gloucestershire 1850. Includes Bristol, Cheltenham, Cirencester, Gloucester, Minchinhampton, Sodbury, Stow, Stroud, Tetbury, Tewkesbury, Wotton. Extracts from *Slater's Gloucestershire directory 1850.*

Hampshire 1851. Includes Andover, Basingstoke, Christchurch, Fareham, Gosport, Havant, Lymington, Portsea, Portsmouth, Romsey, Southampton, Winchester, Isle of Wight, Cowes, Newport, Ryde, Ventnor. Extracts from *Slater's Hampshire directory 1851.*

Herefordshire 1850. Includes Bromyard, Hereford, Kington, Ledbury, Leominster, Pembridge, Ross, Weobley. Extracts from Slater's Herefordshire directory 1850.

Hertfordshire 1846. Includes Baldock, Barnet, Berkhampstead, Bishops Stortford, Cheshunt, Hatfield, Hemel Hempsted, Hertford, Hitchin, Hoddesdon, Rickmansworth, Royton, St.Albans, Tring, Waltham Cross, Ware, Watford. Extracts from *Kelly's Post Office 1846 Herts. directory.*

Huntingdonshire 1847. Includes Godmanchester, Huntingdon, Ramsey, St.Ives, St.Neots. Extracts from *Kelly's Post Office 1847 Huntingdonshire directory.*

Kent 1846. Includes Brompton, Canterbury, Chatham, Cranbourn, Dartford, Deal, Dover, Faversham, Folkestone, Gravesend, Greenwich, Hythe, Lewisham, Maidstone, Margate, Ramsgate, Rochester, Sandwich, Sevenoaks, Sheerness, Sittingbourne, Strood, Tenterden, Tunbridge, Tunbridge Wells, Woolwich. Extracts from *Kelly's Kent Post Office directory 1846.*

Lancashire 1848 (some 1851). Includes Bacup, Birkenhead, Blackburn, Blackpool, Bolton, Bury, Chorley, Clitheroe, Colne, Darwen, Eccles, Fleetwood, Lancaster, Liverpool, Manchester, Oldham, Ormskirk, Preston, Rochdale, St.Helens, Salford, Southport, Todmorden, Ulverston, Warrington, Whalley, Wigan. Extracts from *Slater's Lancashire directory 1848,* & *Mannex & Co's Lancashire directory 1851.*

Leicestershire 1846. Includes Ashby de la Zouch, Castle Donnington, Hinckley, Leicester, Loughborough, Lutterworth, Market Harborough, Melton Mowbray. Extracts from *White's Leicestershire directory 1846.*

Lincolnshire 1856. Includes Alford, Boston, Brigg, Donnington, Gainsborough, Grimsby, Holbeach, Horncastle, Lincoln, Louth, Market Rasen, Sleaford, Spalding, Wainfleet. Extracts from: *White's Lincolnshire directory 1856.*

Middlesex 1846. Includes Bow, Brentford, Clapton, Dalston, Edmonton, Enfield, Finchley, Fulham, Hammersmith, Hampstead, Highgate, Holloway, Hornsey, Stoke Newington, Tottenham, Twickenham, Uxbridge. Extracts from *Kelly's Middlesex Post Office directory 1846.*

Monmouthshire 1850. Includes Abergavenny, Caerleon, Chepstow, Monmouth, Newport, Pontypool, Tredegar. Extracts from *Slater's Monmouth directory 1850.*

Northumberland & Durham 1847 (some 1848). Includes Alnwick, Barnard Castle, Berwick, Chester le Street, Darlington, Durham, Gateshead, Haltwhistle, Hartlepool, Hexham, Newcastle, North Shields, Middlesbrough, Stockton upon Tees, Sunderland. Extracts from *White's Durham directory 1847, White's Northumberland directory 1847, White's Yorkshire directory 1847,* & *Slater's Northumberland directory 1848.*

Norfolk 1846. Includes Kings Lynn, Norwich, North Walsham, South Walsingham, Thetford, Wells, Wymondham, Yarmouth. Extracts from: *Kelly's Post Office 1846 Norfolk directory. White's Norfolk directory 1845.*

Northamptonshire 1849. Includes Brackley, Daventry, Kettering, Northampton, Oundle, Peterborough, Towcester, Wellingborough. Extracts from *White's Northamptonshire 1849 directory.*

Nottinghamshire 1855. Includes Mansfield, Newark, Nottingham, Retford, Sneinton, Southwell, Sutton in Ashfield, Tuxford, Worksop. Extracts from *Post Office Nottinghamshire directory 1855.*

Oxfordshire 1847. Includes Banbury, Bicester, Henley on Thames, Oxford, Thame, Witney. Extracts from *Post Office Oxfordshire directory 1847.*

Rutland 1846. Includes Oakham, Uppingham. Extracts from *White's Rutland directory 1846.*

Shropshire 1842. Includes Bishop's Castle, Bridgnorth, Brossley, Church Stretton, Cleobury Mortimer, Clun, Drayton, Ellesmere, Ludlow, Newport, Oldbury, Oswestry, Shifnall, Shrewsbury, Wellington, Wem, Wenlock, Whitchurch. Extracts from *Pigot's Shropshire 1842.*

Somerset 1848 (some 1850). Includes Bath, Bridgewater, Chard, Collumpton, Crewkerne, Glastonbury, Ilminster, Newton Abbot, Shepton Mallet, Taunton, Teignmouth, Torquay, Totnes, Wellington, Wells, Weston Super Mare, Wincanton, Yeovil. Extracts from *Hunt & co's Bath directory 1848,* & *Hunt's Somerset directory 1848.*

Staffordshire 1851. Includes Bilston, Burslem, Burton on Trent, Cheadle, Dudley, Fenton, Handley, Handsworth, Kingswinford, Leek, Lichfield, Longton, Newcastle under Lyme, Rugeley, Stafford, Sedgley, Stoke upon Trent, Stone, Tamworth, Tipton, Tunstall, Uttoxeter, Walsall, Wednesbury, West Bromwich, Willenhall, Wolverhampton. Extracts from *White's Staffordshire Post Office directory 1851.*

Suffolk 1846. Includes Aldborough, Beccles, Brandon, Bungay, Bury St. Edmnunds, Clare, East Bergholt, Eye, Framlingham, Ipswich, Lowestoft, Mildenhall, Stowmarket, Sudbury, Woodbridge. Extracts from *Kelly's Post Office 1846 Norfolk directory, Kelly's Post Office 1846 Suffolk,* & *Kelly's Essex Post Office directory 1846.*

Surrey 1846. Includes Brixton, Chertsey, Clapham, Croydon, Dorking, Dulwich, Egham, Epsom, Farnham, Godalming, Guildford, Kingston, Mitcham, Norwood, Peckham, Putney, Reigate, Richmond, Stockwell, Wandsworth. Extracts from *Kelly's Surrey Post Office directory 1846.*

Direct Resources (*continued*)

Sussex 1846. Includes Arundel, Battle, Bognor, Brighton, Chichester, Cuckfield, East Grinstead, Eastbourne, Hastings, Horsham, Lewes, Petworth, Rye, St.Leonards, Worthing. Extracts from *Kelly's Sussex Post Office directory 1846.*

Warwickshire 1846. Includes Bilston, Birmingham, Burslem, Fenton, Kingswinford, Longton, Stoke upon Trent, Willenhall, Wolverhampton. Extracts from *White's Warwickshire directory 1850.*

Westmoreland 1851. Includes Appleby, Kendal, Kirkby Stephen, Kirkby Thore. Extracts from *Mannex & Co's Westmoreland directory 1851.*

Wiltshire 1848. Includes Bradford, Calne, Chippenham, Devizes, Malmesbury, Marlborough, Melksham, Salisbury, Swindon, Trowbridge, Warminster. Extracts from *Post Office Wiltshire 1848 directory.*

Worcestershire 1850. Includes Bewdley, Bromsgrove, Droitwich, Dudley, Evesham, Kidderminster, Malvern, Pershore, Redditch, Shipton, Stourbridge, Stourport, Tenbury, Upton, Worcester. Extracts from *Slater's Worcestershire directory 1850.*

Yorkshire 1848 (some 1847). Includes Barnsley, Beverley, Bradford, Doncaster, Driffield, Easingwold, Halifax, Huddersfield, Hull, Keighley, Malton, Mirfield, Northallerton, Otley, Pateley Bridge, Pickering, Pontefract, Ripon, Rotherham, Scarborough, Selby, Skipton, Tadcaster, Thirsk, Wakefield, Whitby, York. Extracts from *White's Yorkshire directory 1847, & Slater's Yorkshire directory 1848.*

Doncaster & District Family History Society

c/o Mrs.J.Wade, 6 Melford Drive, Balby, Doncaster, South Yorkshire, DN4 9AT.
Email: gwenjennings@email.mpn.com
Webpage. www.doncasterfhs.freeserve.co.uk

Doncaster, St.George: burial indexes & M.I's. £15.00 + p&p. 65p (UK); 85p (overseas surface) £1.50 (airmail).

Drake Software Associates

1 Wychwood Rise, Great Missenden, Bucks., HP16 0HB.
Website: www.tdrake.demon.co.uk
Email: barney@tdrake.demon.co.uk

Prices

Prices are inclusive in the U.K. Upgrades are available for owners of versions previous to those listed with an asterisk.

British date calculator. Version 2 CD. £12.00. Shows days of the week from 1000-2050 A.D., Easter, regnal years, census, feast days, quarter days.

Value of the pound. Version 3. 3½" disk. £7.95. Translates the purchasing power of the pound between any two dates from 1600 to 1999. Draws inflation graph between dates.

Bucks Posse Comitatus. Version 2.* CD. £19.95. Listing of 26,000 men in Buckinghamshire in 1798. Search engine and parish mapping of results.

BIRDIE. Version 2.2. CD. £25.00. Turns any GEDCOM or CSV file into event databases that can be searched, sorted, printed and mapped by county and parish (with add-on county pack) BKM map is included.

BIRDIE 2 county disk. Version 2. 3½"disk. £2.50 per county map. (see website for availability). Adds parish mapping to BIRDIE 2 for these counties: BDF., BRK.

2% sample of the U.K. 1851 census. Version 1. CD. Search, sort, print and map by county any entry from the 2% sample from almost all counties.

Pigot's directory, 1830, for Berks, Bucks., Oxon. Version 1. CD. £19.95.

Pigot's directory 1834 for Northumberland and Durham. Version 1. CD. £19.95.

RTF Wizard for the 1881 British census on Cd-Rom. Version 1.03 CD. £9.95. Converts the Rich Text Format (R.T.F.) files from the L.D.S. census export into GEDCOM, CSV, DBF, or DB file formats for spreadsheets/databases.

MACH 1881 census for Bedfordshire. Version 1. CD. £15.00.

MACH 1881 census for Berkshire. Version 1. CD. £15.00.

MACH 1881 census for Buckinghamshire. Version 1. CD. £15.00.

British Isles VRI companion. Version 1. CD. £9.95. Identifies parish registers included on the LDS Vital Records Index CD.

History of Buckinghamshire / George Lipscombe. 4 vols. on CD. Originally published 1846. £20.00.

Eneclann Ltd.

Unit 1b, Trinity College Enterprise Centre, Pearse Street, Dublin 2, Ireland.
Phone: 353 1 6710338
Fax: 353 1 6710281
Email: epubs@eneclann.ie
Webpage: www.eneclann.ie

Index of Irish wills 1484-1858: records at the National Archives of Ireland. £IR36.00.

The William Smith O'Brien petition. £IR36.00. Lists over 80,000 signatories to a petition for clemency for the leader of the 1848 rising.

The Dublin city census 1851. £IR36.00. Forthcoming. List of names from the destroyed census.

Counties in time. Published in association with the National Archives of Ireland. Forthcoming. Introductory guide to 31 classes of records in the National Archives.

The calendars of wills and administrations 1858-1922. Forthcoming. Covers the Dublin (or Principal) Registry area, and including over 1,000,000 names from throughout Ireland in the destroyed wills.

Family History Indexes

Stuart Tamblin, 14, Copper Leaf Close, Moulton, Northampton, NN3 7HS.

Phone: (01604) 495106
Email: fhindexes@genfair.com
Webpage: www.genfair.com/fhindexes

Indexes are also available on fiche.

Criminal register indexes (HO27). [On CD]
- *First series 1805-1816.*

    CDP1. *South-West (Cornwall, Devon, Somerset, & Dorset).* £14.50.

    CDP2. *South Central (Wiltshire, Berkshire & Hampshire).* £14.50.

    CDP3. *London (Middlesex & Surrey).* £14.50.

    CDP4. *South-East (Sussex & Kent).* £14.50.

    CDP5. *Wales & Borders (Wales & Monmouthshire, Shropshire, Herefordshire, Gloucestershire & Bristol).* £14.50.

    CDP6. *Home Counties north (Oxfordshire, Buckinghamshire, Bedfordshire, Hertfordshire, & Essex).* £14.50.

    CDP7. *West Midlands (Staffordshire, Worcestershire & Warwickshire).* £14.50.

    CDP8. *East Midlands (Derbyshire, Nottinghamshire, Lincolnshire, Leicestershire, Rutland, Northamptonshire).* £14.50.

    CDP9. *East Anglia (Huntingdonshire, Cambridgeshire, Norfolk & Suffolk).* £14.50.

    CDP10. *North-West (Lancashire & Cheshire).* £14.50.

    CDP11. *North & North-East (Cumberland, Westmorland, Northumberland, Durham & Yorkshire).* £14.50.

    CDPD. *Death sentences: all counties.* £9.99.

    CDPS. *Serious crimes: all counties.* £9.99.

    CDPT. *Transportation: all counties.* £9.99.

    CDPX. *Surname master index: all counties.* £7.99.

- *Second series 1817-1828.*
    CDP201 *Devon & Cornwall.* £14.50.

Criminal register indexes (HO27) (3½" floppy disks):
- *First series (1805-1816.* Set £127.76.
    Vol. 1. *Somerset & Dorset.* £4.99.
    Vol. 2. *Devon & Cornwall.* £5.99.
    Vol. 3. *Wiltshire.* £3.99.
    Vol. 4. *Gloucestershire & Bristol.* £4.99.
    Vol. 5. *Wales & Monmouthshire.* £3.99.
    Vol. 6. *Oxfordshire & Berkshire.* £3.99.
    Vol. 7. *Northamptonshire, Leicestershire & Rutland.* £3.99.
    Vol. 8. *Buckinghamshire & Hertfordshire.* £3.99.
    Vol. 9. *Bedfordshire, Cambridgeshire & Huntingdonshire.* £3.99.
    Vol.10. *Cumberland, Westmorland, Northumberland & Durham.* £3.99.
    Vol.11. *Middlesex.* £3.99.
    Vol.12. *Hampshire.* £4.99.
    Vol.13. *Derbyshire, Nottinghamshire & Lincolnshire.* £5.99.

Vol.14. *Cheshire.* £3.99.
Vol.15. *Shropshire & Staffordshire.* £4.99.
Vol.16. *Herefordshire & Worcestershire.* £3.99.
Vol.17. *Warwickshire.* £4.99.
Vol.18. *Norfolk & Suffolk.* £6.99.
Vol.19. *Essex.* £5.99.
Vol.20. *Surrey.* £6.99.
Vol.21. *Kent.* £6.99.
Vol.22. *Sussex.* £3.99.
Vol.23. *Lancashire.* £12.99.
Vol.24. *Yorkshire.* £6.99.
Vol.X. *Master index.* £4.99. Shows name & county.
- *Second series (1817-1828).*
Vol.25. *Cornwall.* £3.99.
Vol.26. *Dorset.* £3.99.
Vol.27. *Bedfordshire.* £3.99.
Vol.34. *Devon.* £8.99.
Vol.38. *Bristol.* £3.99.
Vol.45. *Leicestershire.* £4.99.
- *Third series (1829-1840).*
Vol.66. *Cornwall.* £4.99.
Vol.67. *Dorset.* £4.99.
- *1805-1840 series:*
Vol.5A. *Anglesey.* 99p

Militia musters, 1781-82 (WO13) / Liz Hore & Stuart Tamblin.
3½" floppy disks.
Berkshire. £3.99.
Buckinghamshire. £3.99.
Cheshire. £3.99.
Cornwall. £3.99.
Cumberland. £3.99.
Devon East. £3.99.
Devon North. £3.99.
Devon South. £3.99.
Dorset. £3.99.
Durham. £3.99.
Essex East. £3.99.
Essex West. £3.99.
Gloucestershire North. £3.99.
Gloucestershire South. £3.99.
Hampshire North. £3.99.
Hampshire South & I.O.W. £3.99.
Herefordshire. £3.99.
Kent East. £3.99.
Kent West. £3.99.
Lancashire. £3.99.
Leicestershire. £3.99.
Lincolnshire North. £3.99.
Lincolnshire South. £3.99.
Northants & Rutland. £3.99.
Northumberland. £3.99.
Nottinghamshire. £3.99.
Oxfordshire. £3.99.
Shropshire. £3.99.
Somerset. £3.99.
Staffordshire. £3.99.

Surrey. £3.99.
Sussex. £3.99.
Warwickshire. £3.99.
Westmorland. £3.99.
Wiltshire. £3.99.
Worcestershire. £3.99.
Yorkshire East. £3.99.
Yorkshire North 1. £3.99.
Yorkshire West 1. £3.99.
Yorkshire West 2. £3.99.
Anglesey. £3.99.
Brecknockshire. £3.99.
Caernarvonshire. £3.99.
Cardiganshire. £3.99.
Carmarthenshire. £3.99.
Denbighshire. £3.99.
Flintshire. £3.99.
Glamorganshire. £3.99.
Merionethshire. £3.99.
Montgomeryshire. £3.99.
Monmouthshire. £3.99.
Pembrokeshire. £3.99.
Radnorshire. £3.99.

Everton Necropolis (Low Hill Cemetery), Liverpool: Burials 1825-1827. CD. £5.99. Further volumes forthcoming.

PRO Names. 3 3½" floppy disks. £2.50. each. Indexes to miscellaneous personal names in the following Public Record Office classes:

ADM.	Admiralty
AIR.	Air Ministry
AVIA.	Ministry of Aviation
BT.	Board of Trade
CAB.	Cabinet Office
CHES.	Palatinate of Cheshire
CO.	Colonial Office
FO.	Foreign Office
HCA.	High Court of Admiralty
HD.	Secret Intelligence Service
HO.	Home Office
KB.	King's Bench
MEPO.	Metropolitan Police
MH.	Ministry of Helath
MINT.	Royal Mint
PC.	Privy Council
PCOM.	Prison Commission
PIN.	Ministry of Pensions
PMG.	Paymaster General
RAIL.	Railways
RG.	Registrar General
SP.	State Paper Office
T.	Treasury
TS.	Treasury Solicitor
WO.	War Office
ZJ.	*London gazette.*

Prisoners pardoned (HO13-from 1782). CD forthcoming. Vols. currently available are on 3½" floppy disk and fiche:

vol. 1. *28 Nov. 1782 to 19 Mar 1784.* £1.99.
vol.12. *7 June 1798 to 1 July 1801.* £2.99.
vol.13. *3 July 1800 to 19 June 1801.* £2.99.
vol.14. *18 June 1801 to 6 Sept. 1802.* £2.99.
vol.15. *27 Aug. 1802 to 12 July 1803.* £2.99.
vol.16. *3 Jan 1804 to 11 July 1805.* £2.99.

Cornwall Railway (RAIL 134/40). 3½" floppy disk. £2.99. Lists men employed by Cornwall Railways when it was taken over by Great Western Railways in 1889. Expanded version of information in *PRO Names 2.* (see above)

Criminal lunatics (HO20/13) (Bethlem Hospital and County asylums, 1799-1843). 3½" floppy disk. £2.99. Expanded version of information in *PRO Names 2.* (see above)

Courts martial and executions (WO71/344-690. Courts martial 1914-1921; WO93/49. Soldiers executed 1914-1920). 3½" floppy disk. CD under consideration. £2.99. Expanded version of information in *PRO Names.*

The Jutland roll of honour (compiled from official Admiralty sources). 3½" floppy disk. £4.99. Expanded version of information in *PRO Names 2.*

Family History Shop

24d Magdalen Street, Norwich, NR3 1HU.
Phone: (01603) 621151
Email: jenlibrary@aol.com
Webpage: www.jenlibrary.u-net.com/

Please note
Some of the items listed below are also available on fiche.

City of London Maternity Hospital: surname index 1813-March 1840. £10.50.

Great Yarmouth, Norfolk: paupers as to place of settlement ... 1766-1844. £9.00.

Huguenot exiles from Europe 1618-1688 and in the reign of Louis XIV. £18.50.

Sheerness, Kent: dockyard church baptisms 1688-1798, marriages 1744, and burials 1730-1806. £9.00

East Anglian Militia documents list. £29.75. 19th c.; covers Norfolk, Suffolk, Cambridgeshire, Essex and Middlesex. Also available on 3½" floppy disk.

Harrod's directory of Norfolk 1872. £18.50.

Kelly's handbook of the upper ten thousand, 1878. Forthcoming. £18.50.

Family History Shop Library marriage index. Forthcoming. £18.50. Described as a 'potluck' index, covering 1538-1900.

Norfolk miscellanea. Forthcoming. £12.50. Contents: nonconformist burials; Kings Lynn miscellanea, inc. freemen; poor law *etc.*

Norfolk army & militia documents. Forthcoming. £18.50.

Militia attestations indexes to soldier documents:
- *Middlesex Regiment A-Z.* 3½" floppy disk. Ref. 146d. £12.00.
- *Suffolk Regiment & Suffolk RGA.* 3½" floppy disk. Ref. 105d. £7.00.

- *Essex Regiment A-Z.* 3½" floppy disk Ref. 145d. £12.00.
- *Dublin RGA. 1884-1915.* 3½" floppy disk. Ref. 115d. £5.00.
- *Norfolk RGA 1874-1912.* 3½" floppy disk. Ref. 103d. £4.00.
- *Kent RGA 1871-1913.* 3½" floppy disk. Forthcoming.
- *Royal Irish Rifles 1875-1914.* 3½" floppy disk. Forthcoming.
- *East Kent Regiment. 3rd Foot* (The Buffs.) 3½" floppy disk. Ref.174d. •£6.00.
- *S.E. Scotland RGA. Militia documents 1877-1913.* 3½" floppy disk. Ref.173d. £2.50.
- *Essex Regiment Militia documents. 44th Foot.* 3½" floppy disk. £12.00

Norfolk Militia sub-division book 1798-9. 3½" floppy disk. Forthcoming.

City of London Lying in Hospital: baptisms.
    v.1. 1813-part 1821. 3½" floppy disk. Ref. 120d. £3.50.
    v.2. part 1821-1831. 3½" floppy disk. Ref. 121d. £3.50.
    v.3. 1832-Mar. 1840. 3½" floppy disk. Ref. 122d. £3.50.
    v.4. Mar.1840-Sep.1847. 3½" floppy disk. Forthcoming.
    v.5. Sep.1847-Nov.1857. 3½" floppy disk. Forthcoming.

1821 & 1831 Marylebone Census surname index: householders index. £10.50.

Marylebone 1821 census surname index. 3½" floppy disk. Ref. 99d. £5.00.

Marylebone 1831 census surname index. 1841-1891. 3½" floppy disk. Ref.79d. £3.00.

Prerogative Court of Canterbury:
    Norfolk & Suffolk people 1853-7. 3½" floppy disk. Ref.2d. £3.00.
    Norfolk & Suffolk people 1801-1852. A-C. 3½" floppy disk. Ref. 76d. £5.00.
    Norfolk & Suffolk people 1801-1852. D- . 3½" floppy disk. Forthcoming.

Great Yarmouth jail and Bridewell register. 3½" floppy disk. Forthcoming.

Norwich Mercury surnames index, 1780-1784. 3½" floppy disk. Ref.87d. £3.00.

Sheerness Dockyard church baptisms, marriages & burials 1688-1806. Index only. 3½" floppy disk. £5.00.

Norfolk Regiment WO97 army documents with Norfolk Artillery recruits & lieutenants. 3½" floppy disk. £5.00.

Norfolk Regiment WO96 militia attestations. 3½" floppy disk. £5.00.

Family History Society of Cheshire

c/o Graham Fidler, Sedley, Mere Close, Pickmere, Knutsford, Cheshire. WA16 0JR.
Email: grahamfidler@btinternet.com
Webpage: www.fhsc.org.uk\cdrom.htm

Postage
Add £1.50 UK; £3.00 overseas airmail

Bertram Merrell Cheshire marriage index, version 2. £20.00.
    Covers most Cheshire parishes, 1700-1837; also includes Hartley Jones's *Wirral marriage index,* covering c.1550-c.1850. Upgrades of version 1 available for £6.50 and return of the original CD.

Cheshire 25" Ordnance Survey maps, 3rd ed. Originally
   published 1904-10. £30.00
*The history of the County Palatine and City of Chester /
   George Ormerod.* 2nd ed. Originally published 1882.
   Published in association with the Cheshire Local History
   Association
1851 census of Macclesfield. £25.00. Facsimiles of the returns,
   with surname index.
1851 census of Cheshire. Forthcoming.

Federation of Family History Societies

Unit 16, Chesham Industrial Centre, Oram Street, Bury,
Lancs., BL9 6EN
Phone: (0161) 7973843
Fax: (0161) 7973846
Email: orders@ffhs.co.uk
Webpage: www.ffhs.co.uk

Big R 2000. £15.00. Also available on fiche.

National burials index. £30.00. Over 5,300,000 names.

Frith Archive Services

Friths Barn, Teffont, Salisbury, Wiltshire, SP3 5QP.
Email: uksales@francisfrith.com
Webpage: www.francisfrith.co.uk

Frith's photographic directory volume 1. Price on application.
   3,500 vintage photographs of places throughout the British
   Isles
Frith's photographic directory volume 2. Price on application.
   Over 1,100+ Cornish churches and towns.

Genealogy Books

175 Thornton Drive, Fayetteville, GA 30214, U.S.A.
webpage: www.genealogy-books.com
Email: jha@genealogy-books.com

Genealogies / Jeannette Holland Austin. Ref GB.141. $US69.95.
   Or individual families on 3½" floppy discs, $US5.00.
   Includes pedigrees of many British families, including
   Adair/Adare of Ireland, Scotland and America; Bacon of
   Normandy, Suffolk, London & Virginia; Cobb(s) of
   Canterbury, Virgina and Georgia; Conger/Belconger; Hardy
   of Bedfordshire, Isle of Wight, London, and Virginia;
   Hastings of Sussex, Norfolk and Warwickshire; Holland of
   Lancashire, London, Virginia, *etc.,* Moulins, Molyneaux,
   Mollenax of Lancashire; Tillman/Tilghman of Kent; and a
   number of American families.

Genealogical Publishing Company, Inc.,

1001 North Calvert Street, Baltimore, Maryland 21202-3897, U.S.A.

Phone: (410) 837-8271
Fax: (410) 752-8492
Webpage: www.genealogical.com
Available in UK. from TWR Computing (see entry below).

Postage
In U.S.A. add $US3.50 for one CD; $1.25 for each additional CD.

The complete book of emigrants, 1607-1776 / Peter Wilson Coldham. CD #7350. $US29.99. Contents:
  - *Complete book of emigrants.* Originally published in 4 vols, 1987-93.
  - *Complete book of emigrants in bondage, 1614-1775.* Originally published 1988, with 1992 supplement. Details of 140,000 English emigrants.

Early New England settlers, 1600s-1800s. CD#7504. $US39.99. Contents:
  - *The English ancestry and homes of the Pilgrim Fathers / Charles E. Banks.* Originally published 1929.
  - *The Planters of the Commonwealth ... in Massachusetts, 1620-1640 / Charles E. Banks.* Originally published 1930.
  - *The Winthrop fleet of 1630 / Charles E. Banks.* Originally published 1930.
  - *Topographical dictionary of 2885 English emigrants to New England 1620-1650 / Charles E. Banks.* Originally published 1976.
  - 17 other books primarily of New England interest

English origins of New England families, from the New England Historical and Genealogical Register. CD#7181. $US39.99. Notes on 1,500 families and 150,000 individuals.

Notable British families. CD#7367. $US39.99. Contents:
  - *Burke's American families with British ancestry.* 16th ed. Originally published 1939.
  - *The prominent families of the United States.* Originally published 1908.
  - *A genealogical history of the dormant, abeyant, forfeited and extinct peerages of the British Empire.* Originally published 1883.
  - *A genealogical and heraldic history of the extinct and dormant baronetcies of England, Ireland, and Scotland.* Originally published 1841.
  - *The general armory of England, Scotland, Ireland and Wales.* Originally published 1842 or 1878.
  - *A genealogical and heraldic history of the commoners of Great Britain and Ireland.* Originally published 1891-5.
  - *A genealogical and heraldic history of the colonial gentry.*
  - *Burke's family records.*

Lewis's gazetteers of England, Ireland, and Scotland. CD#7270. $US39.99. Contents:
  - *A topographical dictionary of England / Samuel Lewis.* 4 vols. Originally published 19th c.
  - *A topographical dictionary of Ireland / Samuel Lewis.* 2 vols. Originally published 19th c.

- *A topographical dictionary of Scotland / Samuel Lewis.*
  2 vols. Originally published 19th c.

British and American coats of arms. CD#7368. $US29.99.
Contents:
- *The general armory of England, Scotland, Ireland and Wales / John Bernard Burke.* Originally published 1842 or 1878.
- *Fairbairns book of crests of the families of Great Britain / James Fairbairn.* Originally published late 19th c.
- *An ordinary of account of arms contained in the public register of all arms and bearings in Scotland / Sir James Balfour Paul.* Originally published 1893 or 1903.
- *Complete American armory and blue book / John Matthews.*
- *Boltons American armory / Charles Knowles Bolton.* Originally published 1964.
- *Crozier's general armory / William Armstrong Crozier.* Originally published 1904.
- *Virginia heraldica / William Armstrong Crozier.* Originally published 1908.

American source records in England. CD#7364. $US39.99.
Contents:
- *American wills proved in London 1611-1775.* Originally published 1992.
- *American wills and administrations in the Prerogative Court of Canterbury 1610-1857.* Originally published 1989.
- *English estates of American colonists 1610-1699.* Originally published 1980.
- *English estates of American colonists 1700-1799.* Originally published 1980.
- *English estates of American settlers 1800-1858.* Originally published 1981.
- *Genealogical gleanings in England.* 2 vols. Originally published 1901.
- *Virginia gleanings in England.* Originally published 1908.
- *American colonists in English records.* Originally published 1932.
- *English origins of American colonists, from the New York genealogical and biographical record.* Originally published 1932.
- *Topographical dictionary of 2,885 English emigrants to New England.* Originally published 1860.
- *Result of some researches among the British archives ... relative to ... New England.* Originally published 1860.

Irish immigrants to North America. CD#7257. $US29.99.
Contents:
- *Emigrants from Ireland to America 1735-1743: a transcription of the report of the Irish House of Commons into enforced emigration to America.*
- *Irish passenger lists 1803-1806: lists of passengers sailing from Ireland to America.*
- *An alphabetical index to Ulster emigration to Philadelphia 1803-1850.*

- *Passengers from Ireland: lists of passengers arriving at American ports between 1811 and 1817 (transcribed from the Shamrock or Hibernian Chronicle).*
- *Irish emigration lists 1833-1839: lists of emigrants extracted from the Ordnance Survey memoirs for Counties Londonderry and Antrim.*
- *Irish emigration to New England through the Port of Saint John, New Brunswick, Canada, 1841 to 1849.*
- *A list of alien passengers bonded from 1 January 1847 to January 1, 1851, for the use of the Overseers of the Poor in the Commonwealth [Massachusetts].*
- *Emigrants from Ireland, 1847-1852: state-aided emigration schemes from Crown estates in Ireland.*
- *Irish passenger lists 1847-1871: lists of passengers sailing from Londonderry to America on ships of the J. & J. Cooke line and the McCorkell Line.*
- *Irish emigrants in North America [1775-1825].*

An index to Griffith's valuation: a systematic guide to occupiers of property in Ireland between 1848 and 1864. CD#7188. $US59.99.

Tithe Applotment books 1823-1838. CD#7262. $US49.99. For Ireland.

Irish flax growers list 1796. CD#7271. $US29.99. Lists 60,000 individuals.

Irish source records. CD#7275. $US39.99. Contents:
- *A guide to copies and abstracts of Irish wills.*
- *Indexes to Irish wills 1536-1857.*
- *Index to the Prerogative wills of Ireland 1536-1810.*
- *Quaker records, Dublin: abstracts of wills.*
- *Return of owners of land in Ireland 1876.*
- *Irish marriages [from Walkers Hibernian Magazine 1771-1812].*
- *Ireland: 1841-1851 census abstracts (Republic of Ireland).*
- *Ireland: 1841-1851 census abstracts (Northern Ireland).*
- *County Cork, Ireland: a collection of 1851 census records.*

Scottish immigrants to North American 1600s-1800s: the collected works of Donald Dobson. CD#7268. $US39.99. Contents:
- *The original Scots colonists of early America, 1612-1783.*
- Ditto, *supplement 1607-1707.*
- Ditto, *Caribbean supplement 1611-1707.*
- *Directory of Scottish settlers in North America, 1625-1825.* 7 vols.
- *Scots on the Chesapeake 1607-1830.*
- *Scots in the Carolina's 1680-1830.*
- Directory of Scots banished to the American plantations 1650-1775.
- *Scottish soldiers in Colonial America.*
- *Scots in the West Indies 1707-1857.*
- *Scots in the U.S.A. and Canada 1825-1875.*

English settlers in Barbados 1637-1800. CD#7022. $US39.99. Includes 6 volumes of baptisms, marriages and probate records edited by Joanne McRee Sanders.

Genealogical Research Directory

P.O.Box 795, North Sydney, NSW 2059, Australia.
British Agent: Elizabeth Simpson, 2 Stella Grove, Tollerton,
Nottinghamshire. NG12 4EY.

Phone: 0115 9372287
Fax: 0115 9377018
Email: grdxxx@ozemail.com.au
Webpage: www.ozemail.com.au/~grdxxx

Genealogical research directory 1990-1999. £21.00 (inc.p&p).
600,000 research queries listed.

Gensearch

7, Victoria Place, Lymington, Hants. SO41 3TD.

Phone: (01590) 670163
Email: gensearch@lymington.demon.co.uk
Website: www.gensearch co.uk

Beginsearch. 3½" floppy disk. £5.95 (inc p&p). An introduction
to genealogical sources for the beginner.
Army search. 3½" floppy disk. £5.95 (inc p&p). Introduction to
army records.
Hiddensearch. 3½" floppy disk. £5.95 (inc p&p). How to search
for records which are not where they should be. For
experienced researchers.
Irish Search. 3½" floppy disk. £5.95 (inc p&p). Guidance for
the researcher based in England.

Glamorgan Family History Society

c/o Mrs. M. Baird, 1, Dyfed House, Glenside Court, Ty Gwyn
Road, Penylan, Cardiff CF23 5JS.
Webpage: website.lineone.net/-glamfhsoc/

Glamorgan 1851 census. £15.00 (inc. p&p worldwide).

Global Data CD Publishers

1623 W. 3640 South, St.George, UT 84790, U.S.A.
Email: globalcd@infowest.com
Webpage: www.gencd.com/

*Irish vital records CD: Ships passenger lists; Irish wills 1400's-
1800's; 1695 census; Irish of Liverpool 1851.* Ref.CD600A.
$US49.00 + p&p.
Irish wills CD 1400's-1850 / Wallace Clare. Originally
published 1930. Ref.CD804. $US29.00 + p&p. Also available
for down-loading.
Irish of Liverpool 1851 census. Ref.CD501. $US19.95 + p&p.

Heart of Albion Press

2 Cross Hill Close, Wymeswold, Loughborough LE12 6UJ.
Phone: 01509 880725
Fax: 01509 881715
Email: albion@indigogroup.co.uk
Web-page: www.indigogroup.co.uk/albion

Interactive little-known Leicestershire and Rutland / Bob Trubshaw. £14.95. Forthcoming.
Interactive gargoyles and grotesque carvings of Leicestershire and Rutland / Bob Trubshaw. £9.95. Forthcoming. Selection of images from the previous title.
Sepulchral effigies in Leicestershire and Rutland / Max Wade Matthews. £14.95. Forthcoming.

Heraldic Media Ltd

3 Windsor Close, West Norwood, London SE27 9LU.
Phone/Fax: (0)20 8670 3302
Email: info@heraldicmedia.com
Webpage: www.kwtelecom.com/hmedia/webshop

Cracrofts peerage. £47.00 + p&p.

Herefordshire Family History Society

c/o Mr. Alan Charles, 79 College Road, Hereford, HR1 1ED.
Webpage: www.rootsweb.com/~ukhfhs/pubs.html

Monumental inscriptions index. £5.00 + p&p 50p. Index to 51,223 inscriptions for Herefordshire
Ross Registration District burial index 1813-1839. £5.00 + 50p. Also available on fiche.

Heritage Books

1540 Pointer Ridge Place, Bowie, Maryland 20714, USA.
Email: webmaster@heritagebooks.com
Web-page: www.heritagebooks.com

Westmoreland née Neville / Olin V. Mapes. 3rd ed. Item #5061. US25.00. Records of the Westmoreland family of America, and the Neville family of England, 11-20th c.
Heritage Book Archives: English parish records, vol.1. Item #1350. $US32.00. Contents:
  • *The parish registers of St. Antholin, Budge Row, London ... 1538 to 1754 and of St. John Baptist of Wallbrook, London containing the baptisms and burials from 1682 to 1754 / ed. Joseph Lemuel Chester & Geo. J. Armytage (eds.)* Originally published Harleian Society registers 8. 1883.
  • *Index to the first volume of the parish registers of Gainford in the County of Durham, (England). Part I. Baptisms 1560-1784. Part II: Marriages, 1569-1761. Part III. Burials 1569-1784.* Originally published 1889-90.
  • *Little Saxham parish registers; baptisms, marriages and burials ... 1559-1850.* Originally published 1901.
  • *West Stow parish registers 1558-1850, and Wordwell parish registers 1580-1850.* Originally published 1903.

- *Leeds parish church register: first and second books (1571-1612).* Originally published Thoresby Society, 1891.
- *T. Bulmer & Co's history, topography and directory of Lancaster and district / J. Bulmer.* Originally published 1912.

Heritage Book Archives; Ireland, volume 1. Item #1420. $US37.00. Contents:

- *Marriages in the Roman Catholic Diocese of Tuam, Ireland, 1821-1829 / ed. Helen M. Murphy & James R. Reilly.* Covers parts of Co. Mayo, Co. Galway, and Co. Roscommon.
- *Index to the Prerogative wills of Ireland, 1536-1810 / Sir Arthur Vicars.* Originally published 1897.
- *Records relating to the Dioceses of Ardagh & Clonmacnoise / John Canon Monahan.* Originally published 1886.
- *A topographical dictionary of Ireland / Samuel Lewis.* Originally published 1837 or 1840.
- *Appendix to the twenty-sixth report of the Deputy Keeper of the Public Records & Keeper of the State Papers in Ireland.* Originally published 1895. Lists records of the Diocese of Dublin (not the Province).

Heritage Book Archives: Scottish History & Genealogy. Item #1596. $US38.00. Contents:

- *The Scottish nation, volume A-Z / William Anderson.* Originally published 1876. Biographical dictionary.
- *History of the Western Highlands and Isles of Scotland from AD 1493 to A.D. 1625 / Donald Gregory.* Originally published 1836 or 1881.
- *Century of Scottish history / Sir Henry Craik.* Originally published in 2 vols., 1901.
- *Scottish land names: their origin and meaning / Sir Herbert Maxwell.* Originally published 1894.
- *History of the lands and their owners in Galloway / P. A. M'Kerlie.* Originally published 1906.

Heritage Book Archives: the origin and meaning of surnames. Item # 1421. $US31.00. Contents:

- *Genealogy and surnames, with some heraldic and biographical notices / William Anderson.* Originally published 1865.
- *British family names: their origin and meaning / Henry Barber.* 2nd ed. originally published 1903.
- *English surnames: their sources and significations / Charles Wareing Bardsley.* 6th ed. originally published 1898.
- *Family names and their story / S. Baring-Gould.* Originally published 1910.
- *Personal and family names: a popular monograph on the origin and history of the nomenclature of the present and former times / Harry Alfred Long.* Originally published 1883.
- *The origin and signification of Scottish surnames, with a vocabulary of Christian names / Clifford Stanley Sims.* Originally published 1862.
- *Clues to our family names / Lou Stein.* Originally published 1998.

Heritage Book Archives: Heraldry vol.1. Item #1674. $US40.00.
Contents:
- *A display of heraldry / William Newton.* Originally published 1846.
- *The General armory of England, Scotland, Ireland and Wales, comprising a registry of armorial bearings from the earliest to the present time / Sir Bernard Burke.* Originally published 1884.
- *An alphabetical dictionary of coats of arms belonging to families in Great Britain and Ireland, forming an extensive ordinary of British arms / John Papworth, et al.* Originally published 1874.
- *Fairbairn's book of crests of the families of Great Britain and Ireland / James Fairbairn, et al.* 4th ed., originally published 1905.
- *Subject index to Fairbairns book of crests / A. R. Dickins.*

Heritage Book Archives: Ireland, vol.2. Item #1649. $US44.00.
Contents:
- *Ireland: its scenery, character and history / S. C. Hall.* 6 vols. Originally published 1911.
- *Visitation of Ireland / Frederick Arthur Crisp & Joseph Jackson Howard.* 6 vols. Originally published 1897-1918. Collection of pedigrees, not to be confused with the official heraldic visitations.
- *Topographical dictionary of Ireland / Nicholas Carlisle.* Originally published 1810.

Heritage World

The Heritage Centre. Pomeroy Road, Donaghmore, Co.Tyrone, N.Ireland, BT70 3HG.
Phone: (028) 8776 1306
Fax: (028) 8776 7663

The tithe applotment books (Northern Ireland). £35.00. Tithe applotment books, compiled in the 1820's, list all those paying tithe to the established church. This CD lists 200,000 names from 223 parishes in the 6 counties of Northern Ireland.

Index to Flaxgrowers List. £20.00. 60,000 individuals who received a grant for growing flax in 1796 are listed, by parish and county, on this CD.

An index to Griffith's Valuation of Ireland. £40.00. Griffiths valuation is a survey of all property-holders in mid-19th c. Ireland. This CD lists c.1,250,000 names.

Hidden Heritage

Mrs.E.Jack, 11 Old Cheltenham Road, Longlevens, Gloucester, GL2 OAS.
Phone/Fax: 01452 503831
Email: ejack@gloster.demon.co.uk
Webpage: www.gloster.demon.co.uk

Glorious Gloucestershire. 4 CD's. £15.00 (incl.p&p.) per CD.
Contents:
v.1. North and East Gloucestershire: the North Cotswolds
v.2. The Severn Vale: Gloucester, Cheltenham and Tewkesbury.

v.3. The Forest of Dean and the Leadon Vale.
v.4. South Gloucestershire: South Cotswolds and the
Berkeley Vale.
Each CD includes over 1,000 photographs, including every
parish church, and much else.

History Data Services
UK Data Archive, University of Essex, Wivenhoe Park,
Colchester, CO4 3SQ
Webpage: hds.essex.ac.uk
Email: hds@essex.ac.uk
Phone: (0)1206 872003

*Historic Parishes of England & Wales: an electronic map of
boundaries before 1850, with a gazeteer and metadata.*
ISBN: 0-9540032-0-9. £12.95.

i-C.D. Publishing (U.K.) Ltd.
50, Sulivan Road, London SW6 3DX.
Phone: 020 79092180
Email: info@192.com
Webpage: www.192.com

UK-Info Professional. £229.95
UK-Info Disk. £49.95.
UK-Info Home. £29.95.
All these titles include the latest electoral roll, BT/OSIS
database and business listings. The difference in price reflects
varying levels of access, e.g. on the Professional version it is
possible to search by street, partial postcode, etc.

Ibertek
T.C.Waters, 9 Prospect Place, Whitby, North Yorkshire
YO22 4AD.
Email: Ibertek@tcwaters.free-online.co.uk
Webpage: www.tcwaters.free-online.co.uk

Whitby, North Yorkshire, residents & traders 1899. With
*Whitby, North Yorkshire, residents of villages, farms &
country areas, 1899.* 3½" floppy disk. Ref. D1 & D2. £20.00
in Europe; £22.00 elsewhere.
Whitby, North Yorkshire, directory of tradesmen 1823. Ref.
D3. 3½" floppy disk. £10.00 in Europe, £12.00 elsewhere
Whitby past and present / R. B. Holt. Originally published in
2 vols., 1897. 3½" floppy disk. Ref. D4. £15.00 in Europe;
£17.00 elsewhere.
Beverley & district residents 1823. 3½" floppy disk. Ref. D6.
£10.00 in Europe; £12.00 elsewhere.
Bridlington & district residents 1823. 3½" floppy disk. Ref. D7.
£10.00 in Europe; £12.00 elsewhere.
Residents of Whitby, North Yorkshire, in the 1700's. 3½"
floppy disk. Ref. D8. £13.00 in Europe; £15.00 elsewhere.
Information drawn from a variety of sources.
*Kingston upon Hull burials & monumental inscriptions
1600/1700's.* 3½" disk. Ref D9. £10.00 in Europe; £12.00
elsewhere. Drawn from Gent's *History of Hull,* originally
published 1735, and including Holy Trinity, St. Mary's, and
Cave.

Australian convicts & early settlers. 3½" floppy disk. Ref. D10. £25.00 in Europe; £27.00 elsewhere. Extensive listing drawn from a variety of sources.

Ibertek guide to old trades, titles & occupations. 3½" floppy disk. Ref. D11. £13.00 in Europe; £15.00 elsewhere.

Residents of Holbeach (Lincs) & district, 1500s/1600's. 3½" floppy disk. Ref. D12. £13.00 in Europe; £15.00 elsewhere. Births, marriages and deaths.

Shipping records (including names of ships masters & ports of origin.) 1299-1300. Liber Cotidanus. 3½" floppy disk. Ref. D13. £10.00 in Europe; £12.00 elsewhere. Transcript of a manuscript written in 1299-1300, made in 1787. *Liber cotidanus* is an account book of King Edward during his Scottish wars.

Directory of Scarborough & surrounding villages 1823. 3½" floppy disk. Ref. D14. £13.00 in Europe; £15.00 elsewhere.

Directory of Scarborough & surrounding villages 1823. 3½" floppy disk. Ref. D14. £13.00 in Europe; £15.00 elsewhere.

Directory of Bradford on Avon (Wilts) 1899. 3½" floppy disk. Ref. D15. £5.00 in Europe; £7.00 elsewhere.

Directory of York & district 1823. 3½" floppy disk. Ref. D16. £13.00 in Europe; £15.00 elsewhere.

2,000+ British emigrants to North America 1635-1850. 3½" floppy disk. Ref. D17. £13.00 in Europe; £15.00 elsewhere.

Directory of Tadcaster 1890. 3½" floppy disk. Ref. D18. £5.00 in Europe; £7.00 elsewhere.

North Ormesby (Middlesbrough) register of baptisms, marriages & burials 1873 & 1876. 3½" floppy disk. £10.00 in Europe; £12.00 elsewhere.

Residents of Monmouth, Wales 1901. 3½" floppy disk. Ref. D20. £10.00 in Europe; £12.00 elsewhere. Despite the title, Monmouth was in England in 1901, not Wales.

Residents of Filey 1822-1892. 3½" floppy disk. Ref. D21. £10.00 in Europe; £12.00 elsewhere.

Directory of Douglas, Isle of Man; 1823. 3½" floppy disk. Ref. D22. £10.00 in Europe; £12.00 elsewhere.

Residents of Limerick 1769. 3½" floppy disk. Ref. D23. £12.00 in Europe; £15.00 elsewhere.

Ibertek guide to British & Irish pirates. 3½" floppy disk. Ref. D24. £13.00 in Europe; £15.00 elsewhere.

Ilfracombe residents and traders 1850. 3½" floppy disk. Ref. D25. £10.00 in Europe; £12.00 elsewhere.

Black sheep: executed criminals & their victims 1541-1908. 3½" floppy disk. Ref. D20. £13.00 in Europe; £15.00 elsewhere.

Directory of Newport Pagnell traders 1839. Ref. D27. £5.00 in Europe; £7.00 elsewhere.

North country criminal records (relating to Yorkshire, Durham, Cumberland & Northumberland), early 1700's to late 1800's. Ref. D28. £10.00 in Europe; £12.00 elsewhere.

Directory of Knaresborough traders 1822. 3½" floppy disk. £10.00 in Europe; £12.00 elsewhere.

Miscellaneous Yorkshire births 1700-1900. 3½" floppy disk. Ref. D30. £13.00 in Europe; £15.00 elsewhere.

Directory of Ilfracombe traders 1830. 3½" floppy disk. Ref. D31. £5.00 in Europe; £7.00 elsewhere.

Directory of Matlock & Matlock Bath 1857. 3½" floppy disk. Ref. D32. £10.00 in Europe; £12.00 elsewhere.

Directory of Stroud & district 1830. 3½" floppy disk. Ref. D33.
£5.00 in Europe; £7.00 elsewhere. 450 entries, based on
Pigot's directory.

Directory of Buckingham 1839. 3½" floppy disk. Ref. D34.
£5.00 in Europe; £7.00 elsewhere.

Miscellaneous Sheffield residents 1500's to 1900's. 3.½" floppy
disk. Ref. D35. £13.00 in Europe; £15.00 elsewhere. From a
wide variety of sources.

Ramsey (Isle of Man) traders 1837. 3½" floppy disk. Ref. D36.
£10.00 in Europe; £12.00 elsewhere.

Belper (Derbyshire) directory 1835. 3½" floppy disk. Ref. D37.
£10.00 in Europe; £12.00 elsewhere.

Culloden Jacobites. 3½" floppy disk. Ref. D38. £5.00 in Europe;
£7.00 elsewhere. List of 150 supporters of the Stuart cause
in 1745.

Glasgow notables, officers dignitaries & merchants, 1786/1787.
3½" floppy disk. Ref. D39. £13.00 in Europe; £15.00 elsewhere.

Castletown, Isle of Man (including Malew & Ballasalla) 1837.
3½" floppy disk. Ref. D40. £10.00 in Europe; £12.00
elsewhere. Directory.

Isle of Axholme Family History Society

c/o Mr.J.G.Fox, 1 Vinegarth, Epworth, Doncaster, DN9 1SW.
Webpage: www.linktop.demon.co.uk/axholme/advert.htm

*Marriage index database program, with Isle of Axholme
marriage indexes.* 2 C.D's. £1.50 + £3.00 per index. Indexes
as follows:

AM1	Amcotts	1836-1915
BL3	Belton	1542-1659
BL1	Belton	1660-1753
BL2	Belton	1754-1812
CR1	Crowle	1579-1645
EP1	Epworth	1564-1708
EP2	Epworth	1710-1812
HX1	Haxey	1572-1672
HX2	Haxey	1673-1812
KA1	Keadby with Althorpe	1672-1812
LD1	Luddington	1700-1837
OW1	Owston Ferry	1599-1749
OW2	Owston Ferry	1750-1837
WR1	Wroot	1573-1837

Isle of Wight Family History Society

Robin & Shirley Thornton, The Old Rectory, Ashknowle Lane,
Whitwell, Isle of Wight, PO38 2PP.
Email: thorn.wood@virgin.net
Webpage: www.dina.clara.net/iowfhs

System Requirements

Must be able to read large data files in dBASE IV format

Isle of Wight burial index pt.1. Almost 60,000 burials. Ref.
CDRO1. £18.00.

Isle of Wight burial index pt.2. Continuation to 1900/2000.
Ref. CDRO9. £18.00.

Isle of Wight burial index, mid-19th c. to 2000. Ref. CDR10.
£20.00.

County petty sessions CPS1-19, + coroners inquests. Ref. CDR04. £18.00.

Newport petty sessions 1837-1888. Ref. CDR07. £18.00.

1933 electoral register for whole Isle of Wight. Ref. CDR02. £18.00.

1947 electoral register for whole Isle of Wight. Ref. CDR08. £18.00.

Index to 1891 Navy list & 1895 army list. Ref. CDR05. £18.00.

Submarine attacks WW2 + crew lists & pictures. Ref. CDR03. £18.00.

1922 Navy lists: 15,000 names. Ref. CDR06. £18.00.

Index to R.A.F. retired officers lists 1990 - 26,000 names. Ref. CDR11. £18.00.

Index to R.A.F. retired officers lists 1992. Ref. CDR12. Price not given.

Kent Family History Society

c/o Derek Maytum, Stables Cottage, Worthing, Dereham,
  Norfolk, NR20 5HRS.
Phone: (01362) 668754
Website: www.canterhill.co.uk/kfhs
Email: derek.maytum@btinternet.com

Prices
These include UK p&p. Add £0.75 for airmail overseas.

Members Interests directory 1999. Cd-ROM 01. £6.50 members; £7.50 non-members

Parish Registers. CD 02/03. £10.00 members; £15.00 non-members. Contents:
- Ashford St.Mary baptisms 1688-1795, marriages 1693-1780; burials 1693-1795.
- Badlesmere baptisms 1564-1837; marriages 1563-1837; burials 1563-1837.
- Benenden baptisms 1709-1906; marriages 1701-1836; burials 1710-1906.
- Biddenden baptisms 1538-1837; marriages 1538-1837. burials 1538-1877.
- Boughton-u-Blean baptisms 1784-1812.
- Cranbrook baptisms 1558-1812.
- East Peckham baptisms 1558-1812; marriages 1558-1812; burials 1558-1812.
- East Sutton marriages 1648-1812.
- Hollingbourne marriages 1556-1837.
- Leaveland baptisms 1558-1837; marriages 1554-1863; burials 1591-1837.
- Lydd All-Saints baptisms 1801-1846; burials 1800-1812.
- River baptisms 1566-1840; marriages 1566-1837; burials 1556-1840.
- Sellindge marriages 1559-1812.
- Smarden baptisms 1563-1812; marriages 1559-1837; burials 1539-1812.
- Snargate marriages 1552-1837.
- Stourmouth baptisms 1794-1865; marriages 1754-1836.
- Sutton Valence baptisms 1661-1679, 1724-1795; marriages 1577-1836; burials 1661-1679, 1795-1812.

- Swalecliffe baptisms 1558-1850; marriages 1607-1837; burials 1607-1840.
- Yalding baptisms 1559-1579, marriages 1559-1579; burials 1559-1579.

Leicestershire & Rutland Family History Society

101 High Street, Leicester, LE1 4JB.
Email: chairman.lrfhs@ntlworld.com
Website: www.lrfhs.co.uk

Leicester borough 1851 census index. £19.99 + 50p p&p (UK); £1.50 p&p (overseas airmail).
Leicestershire and Rutland burials CD. Volume 1. 1813 to 1865. £19.99 + p&p 50p (UK); £1.50 (overseas airmail).
The church of St. Margaret's, Leicester. Marriages 1837-1897. £19.99 + p&p 50p (UK); £1.50 (overseas airmail).

Lincolnshire Archives

St. Rumbold Street, Lincoln, LN2 5AB.
Phone: (01522) 526204
Email: archive@lincolnshire.gov.uk
Fax: (01522) 525158
Webpage: www.lincolnshire.gov.uk/archives

Lincolnshire Archives guide to collections: archivists reports and accessions 1948-1997. £9.50 + p&p £1.00 (UK); £3.00 (overseas)
Indexes, genealogical resources, and Foster library. £9.50 + p&p £1.00 (UK); £3.00 overseas. Contents:
- Sources for genealogy (summary listing).
- Parish registers fiche index.
- Wills & Admons indexes to Lincoln Consistory Court 1801-58.
- Stow Archdeaconry Court 1700-1834, and Lincoln Probate Registry 1858-1905.
- Convicts sent to Australia index 1787-1840.
- Motor Vehicle licensing FE & VL plates.
- Foster Library catalogue (part).
Indexes of wills 1700-1900. £17.50 + p&p £1.00 (UK); £3.00 (overseas). Includes:
- Stow Archdeaconry Court, 1700-1834.
- Lincoln Consistory Court 1701-1800 & 1801-58.
- Lincoln Probate Registry 1858-1900.

Guy Martin

Willshaw, Whitehough, Chinley, High Peak, SK23 6EJ.
Phone: (01663) 750506
Fax: (01663) 751288
Email: martinguy@aol.com
Webpage: members.aol.com/martinguy/intro/htm

System Requirements
Word 97 or later

Martin & Timothy family histories. £4.50 + p&p (UK 75p; Europe £1.25; U.S.A. £1.75; Rest of world £2.25.)

Adam Mathew Publications

8 Oxford Street, Marlborough, Wiltshire SN8 1AP.
Phone: (01672) 511921
Fax: (01672) 511663

The 1836 national tithe files database. £95.00 + VAT & p&p.

Linda Moorhouse

Elsinore House, 76 Scotforth Road, Lancaster LA1 4SF.
Phone: (01524) 65088
Email: elsinorehs@email.com
Webpage: www.elsinore 99.freeserve.co.uk/lancastercd

North Lancashire from newspapers, directories and other references, 1665 to 1920. £15.00 + p&p £1.00 (UK); £2.00 (overseas). Contents:
- *The diary of William Stout 1665 to 1752.*
- *The gude auld towne of Lancaster in 1803.*
- *The loyal town of Lancaster in 1803.*
- *Peace in Lancaster in 1814.*
- *The assize town of Lancaster in 1821.*
- *A genteel family's tour of Lancaster & the Lake District in 1827.*
- *The ancient borough of Lancaster in 1831.*
- *The good old town of Lancaster in 1841.*
- *On the banks of the River Lune, 1801 to 1840.*
- *The villages of the Lune Valley and estuary, 1841 to 1845.*
- *The opening of Ripley Hospital, Lancaster in 1864.*
- *Scotforth village 1801 to 1845.*
- *The Scotforth murder in 1866.*
- *Directory of Lancaster & district circa 1880.*
- *A guide to Lancaster.* Originally published 1920.

Directories of Westmorland 1849 & 1885; Cumberland 1901. £15.00 + p&p £1.00 (UK); £2.00 (overseas).

A.J.Morris

Postal Address not available.
Webpage: www.genealogy.org/≈ajmorris/catalog/cd.htm
Email: ajmorris@ajmorris.com

Irish Memorials of the Dead. CD1. $US39.00. Contents:
- *Journal of the Association for the Preservation of the Memorials of the Dead, Ireland: consolidated index of surnames and placenames to volumes I-VII (1888-1909).* Originally published Dublin, 1914.
- *Fund for the Preservation of the Memorials of the Dead, Ireland, vols. I-III, 1888-1895/7.*

Indexes to Irish wills. CD2 $US29.00. Contents:
- *Index to the Prerogative wills of Ireland, 1536-1810 / Sir Arthur Vicars (ed.)* Originally published Dublin, 1897.
- *Indexes to Irish wills, vol.I: Ossory, Leighlin, Ferns, Kildare / W.P.W.Phillimore (ed.)* Originally published 1909.
- *Indexes to Irish wills, vol.II: Cork and Ross, Cloyne / W.P.W.Phillimore (ed.)* Originally published 1910.

- *Indexes to Irish wills, vol.III: Cashel and Emly, Waterford and Lismore, Killaloe and Kilfenora, Limerick, Ardfert and Aghadoe / Gertrude Thrift (ed.)* Originally published 1913.
- *Indexes to Irish Wills, vol.IV: Dromore, Newry and Mourne / Gertrude Thrift (ed.)* Originally published 1918.
- *Indexes to Irish wills, vol.V: Derry & Raphoe / Gertrude Thrift (ed.)* Originally published 1920.

Griffith's valuation for County Mayo. CD3. $US44.00. Contents:
- *Index to Griffith's valuation for County Mayo / Andrew J.Morris.*
- *Griffith's valuation for County Mayo / Sir Richard Griffith (ed.)*
- Mayo portion of the *Topographical dictionary of Ireland / Samuel Lewis.* Originally published Dublin, 1837.
- *O'Hart's Irish pedigrees.* CD4. $US33.00.

Irish genealogy. CD5. $US25.00. Contents:
- *Special report on surnames in Ireland, with notes as to numerical strength, derivation, ethnology and distribution / Robert E. Matheson.* Originally published Dublin, 1909.
- *Irish local names explained / P.W.Joyce.* Originally published Dublin, 1902.
- *Concise dictionary of Irish biography / John E.Crone.* Originally published Dublin, 1937.
- *Landowners in Ireland: owners of one acre and upwards, 1876.*

County Mayo chronicles and history. CD6. $US45.00. Contents:
- *County Mayo chronicles / A.J.Morris.*
- *History of County Mayo to the close of the 16th century / H.T.Knox.* Originally published Dublin, 1908.
- *Erris in the Irish Highlands / P.Knight.* Originally published Dublin, 1836.
- Mayo portion of *Topographical dictionary of Ireland / Samuel Lewis.* Originally published Dublin, 1837.

My Family.com
See Ancestry.com

Naval & Military Press Ltd.
Order Dept., Unit 10, Ridgewood Industrial Park, Uckfield, East Sussex, TN22 5QE.

Phone: (01825) 749494
Fax: (01825) 765701
Email: order.dept@naval-military-press.co.uk
Webpage: www.naval-military-press.co.uk

System Notes
Demo versions are available online.

Soldiers died in the Great War 1914-19. Order no. CD01. £220.00 + V.A.T. £38.50. Contents: CD version of 81 published volumes.

Army roll of Honour, World War II: soldiers died in the Second World War, 1939-45. Order no. CD02. £145.00 + V.A.T. £25.38. CD version of the War Office roll of honour, WO304.

Armies of the Crown. Order no. CD03. £38.00 + V.A.T. £6.65. Contents: CD version of published bibliographies by Arthur S. White and Roger Perkins, listing published corps and regimental histories of the British Army and the armies of the British and Indian Empires.

Val Neal

50 Main Street, Middleton, Matlock, Derbyshire, DE4 4LU.
Phone: (10629) 823328
Email: Valerie@actaeon.freeserve.co.uk
Webpage: www.btinternet.com/ivor.neall

Index to Darley Dale parish registers (St.Helens). £12.50 (U.K.); £13.50 overseas. Contents: baptisms 1564-1837; burials 1539-1904 (including South Darley 1846-1918); marriages 1541-1860.
Index to Ashover parish registers (All Saints). £15.00 (UK); £16.00 overseas. Contents: baptisms 1621-1837; burials 1659-1910; marriages 1653-1860.
Index to Matlock parish registers (St.Giles). £12.50 (UK); £13.50 overseas. Contents: baptisms 1638-1837; burials 1637-1910; marriages 1637-1860.

Northumbrian Research

11, River View, Lynemouth, Morpeth, Northumberland, NE61 5TY.
Phone: (01670) 860239
Email: malcolmf@morpeth58.freeserve.co.uk

Postage
Add £1.50 in UK, £2.25 for Europe, £2.75 for North America, £3.00 for Australia.

Bulmers 1886 history, topography and directory of Northumberland, (Hexham Division). £11.99 + p&p.
Bulmers 1887 history, topography and directory of Northumberland (Tyneside, Wansbeck and Berwick Divisions). £11.99 + p&p.
Whellan's 1894 history, topography and directory of the County Palatine of Durham. £11.99 + p&p.
Bulmer's 1901 history, topography and directory of Cumberland. £11.99 + p&p.
White's 1838 history gazetteer and directory of the West Riding of Yorkshire. £11.99 + p&p.
Slater's 1851 trade directory of Staffordshire. £11.99 + p&p.
William West's 1830 history, topography and directory of Warwickshire. £11.99 + p&p.
William White's 1854 history gazetteer and directory of Norfolk. £11.99 + p&p.
Antiquities of the City of Exeter / Richard Izacke. Originally published 1696. £14.99.
Haworth past & present / J. Horsfall Turner. Originally published 1879. £11.99.
Wilson's handbook to Morpeth and neighbourhood. Originally published 1884. £4.95 + p&p; £1.50 (UK); £1.85 (world-wide surface).

Open University

Faculty Offices (CDRom order), Faculty of Social Sciences,
Open University, Milton Keynes, MK7 6AA.
Webpage: www.open.cc.uk/socialsciences/sociology/courses/da301

CDROM archive of research reports in family and community
history. CDR0008 £9.50; later CD's £12.50. Each annual CD
contains hundreds of reports compiled by student researchers
on O.U.course DA301: studying family and community history:
19th and 20th centuries. CD's are available as follows:
   1994 CDR0008. 482 reports
   1995 CDR00015. 389 reports
   1996 CDR0057. 352 reports
   1997 CD0094. 231 reports
   1998 CD0133. 197 reports
   1999 CDR0 232 Forthcoming

Original Indexes

113, East View, Wideopen, Tyne & Wear, NE13 6EF.
Phone: (0191) 2366416
Email: fiche@original-indexes.demon.co.uk
Webpage: www.original-indexes.demon.co.uk/index.htm
All publications on CD are also available as fiche.

Price

Add £1.50 p&p to all orders.

Hodgson's history of Northumberland / John Hodgson.
   Originally published 1820-35. 7 CD's. The set £120.00. Also
   available separately:
   Pt.1, vol.1. General history. Originally published 1827.
      £19.99.
   Pt.2, vol.1. Includes Franchise of Redesdale, and of
      Umfreville family, also parishes in the Deanery of
      Morpeth. Originally published 1832. £19.99.
   Pt.2, vol.2. Includes Morpeth Ward and Castle Ward.
      Originally published 1827. £19.99.
   Pt.2, vol.3. Includes Corbridge and the Franchise and Ward
      of Tindal. Originally published 1840. £19.99.
   Pt.3, vol.1. Includes ancient records and historical papers.
      Originally published 1826. £19.99.
   Pt.3, vol.2. Includes ancient records and historical papers.
      Originally published 1828. £19.99.
   Pt.3, vol.3. Includes ancient records and historical papers.
      Originally published 1835. £19.99.
History and antiquities of North Durham / James Raine.
   Originally published 1852. £19.99. Covers Bedlingtonshire,
   Islandshire, and Norhamshire - all detached portions of
   Co.Durham incorporated into Northumberland in 1844.
The history of the borough, castle and barony of Alnwick /
   George Tate. Originally published in 2 vols., 1866-9. £39.99.
The Northumberland county history. Originally published
   1893-1940. 15 CD's. £230.40 the set, or available separately:
   vol.1. *Bamburgh & Belford.* 1893. £19.99.
   vol.2. *Embleton, Ellingham, Howick, Long Houghton &*
      Lesbury. 1895. £19.99.

vol.3. *Hexhamshire pt.I.* 1896. £19.99.

vol.4. *Hexhamshire, pt.II, with Chollerton, Kirkheaton & Thockrington.* 1897. £19.99.

vol.5. *Warkworth, Shilbottle & Brainshaugh.* 1899. £19.99.

vol.6. *Bywell St.Peter, Bywell St.Andrew, & Slaley.* 1902. £19.99.

vol.7. *Edlingham, Felton, & Brinkburn.* 1904. £19.99.

vol.8. *Tynemouth.* 1907. £19.99.

vol.9. *Earsdon & Horton.* 1909. £19.99.

vol.10. *Corbridge.* 1914. £19.99.

vol.11. *Carham, Branxton, Kirknewton, Wooler & Ford.* 1922. £19.99.

vol.12. *Ovingham, Stamfordham & Ponteland.* 1926. £19.99.

vol.13. *Heddon-on-the-Wall, Newburn, Longbenton, Wallsend, Gosforth, Cramlington, & Newcastle townships (Benwell, Elswick, Heaton, Byker, Fenham & Jesmond).* 1930. £19.99.

vol.14. *Alnham, Chatton, Chillingham, Eglingham, Ilderton, Ingram, Whittingham, Lowick & Doddington.* 1935. £19.99.

vol.15. *Simonburn, Humshaugh, Bellingham, Falstone, Thorneyburn, Greystead, Wark, Rothbury & Alwinton with Holystone & Kidland.* 1940. £19.99.

Newcastle upon Tyne Records Committee publications vol.IX. A volume of miscellanea. Originally published 1930. £14.99. Contents:

- 'List of transcripts partly in manuscript, of the parish register of Northumberland and Durham in the Public Library, Newcastle upon Tyne';
- List of J. C. Hodgson's ms. 'pedigrees of families in Northumberland and Durham'.
- 'Selections from the Delaval papers in the Newcastle upon Tyne Public Library';
- 'The Registers of the Ballast Hills cemetery, Newcastle upon Tyne'.

Berwick upon Tweed: the history of the town and guild / John Scott. Originally published 1888. £19.99.

Data diskettes

Whitburn bap., mar., & bur. 1813-1837 / C. Yellowley (ed.) 3½" floppy disk. £10.00 (inc. p&p).

Longbenton bap., mar., & bur. 1813-1837 / G. Bell (ed.) Disk 22. 3½" floppy disk. £10.00 (inc. p&p).

Marriage indexes / W. E. Rounce. 20 3½" floppy disks. Contents:

Co.Durham

Disk 1. *Auckland St. Helen (1653-1837); Croxdale (1732-1837); Escombe (1543-1837); Hamsterly (1580-1837); Merrington (1579-1837); Shildon (1834-1837); Witton-le-Wear (1558-1837).* 3½" floppy disk. £5.00 (inc. p&p).

Disk 2. *Cockfield (1579-1837); Gainford (1569-1837); Middleton-in-Teesdale (1621-1837); Staindrop (1626-1837); Whorlton (1713-1837); Winston (1716-1837).* 3½" floppy disk. £5.00 (inc. p&p).

Disk 3. *Chester-le-Street (1582-1837); Lamesley (1689-1837); Washington (1603-1837).* 3½" floppy disk. £5.00 (inc. p&p.)

Disk **4**. *Coniscliffe (1590-1837); Denton (1673-1837); Heighington (1571-1837); Hurworth (1560-1837); Middleton St. George (1616-1838); Sockburn (1593-1837).* 3½" floppy disk. £5.00 (inc. p&p.)

Disk **5**. *Brancepeth (1599-1837); Durham St. Margaret (1558-1837); Durham St. Nicholas (1540-1837).* 3½" floppy disk. £5.00 (inc. p&p.)

Disk **6**. *Durham Cathedral (1609-1896); Durham St. Mary le Bow (1573-1837); Durham St. Mary South Bailey (1559-1841); Durham St. Oswald (1538-1837); Pittington (1575-1837); Sherburn Hospital (1695-1766); Witton Gilbert (1568-1837).* 3½" floppy disk. £5.00 (inc. p&p.).

Disk **7**. *Castle Eden (1698-1837); Dalton-le-Dale (1653-1837); Easington (1570-1837); Elwick Hall (1592-1839); Greatham (1564-1837); Monk Hesledon (1592-1837); Seaham (1652-1837).* 3½" floppy disk. £5.00 (inc. p&p.)

Disk **8**. *Gateshead (1559-1837); Gateshead Fell (1825-1837).* 3½" floppy disk. £5.00 (inc. p&p.).

Disk **9**. *Ryton (1581-1837); Whickham (1579-1837).* 3½" floppy disk. £5.00 (inc. p&p.)

Disk **10**. *Hetton-le-Hole (1832-1837); Houghton-le-Spring (1563-1837); Penshaw (1754-1837); West Rainton (1827-1837).* 3½" floppy disk. £5.00 (inc. p&p.)

Disk **11**. *Boldon (1573-1837); South Shields St. Hilda (1653-1837).* 3½" floppy disk. £5.00 (inc. p&p.)

Disk **12**. *South Shields St. Hilda (1837-1901); South Westoe St. Michael (1882-1908).* 3½" floppy disk. £5.00 (inc. p&p.)

Disk **13**. *Hedworth St. Nicholas (1882-1910); Heworth (1696-1837); Jarrow Grange Christ Church (1869-1900); Jarrow Grange Good Shepherd (1893-1949); Jarrow St. Mark (1896-1948); Jarrow St. Peter (1881-1923); South Shields St. Aidan (1888-1910); South Shields St. Jude (1887-1914).* 3½" floppy disk. £5.00 (inc. p&p.)

Disk **14**. *Ebchester (1619-1837); Edmundbyers (1764-1837); Esh (1754-1903); Heathery Cleugh (1828-1837); Hunstanworth (1770-1837); Medomsley (1608-1837); Muggleswick (1755-1837); St.John's Chapel (1828-1837); Satley (1574-1837); Stanhope (1613-1837); Wolsingham (1655-1837).* 3½" floppy disk. £5.00 (inc. p&p.)

Disk **15**. *Aycliffe (1560-1837); Bishopton (1653-1837); Bishop Middleham (1559-1837); Egglecliffe (1540-1837); Embleton (1653-1752); Great Stainton (1561-1837); Kelloe (1693-1837); Long Newton (1564-1837); Redmarshall (1560-1837); Sedgefield (1581-1837); Trimdon (1720-1837).* 3½" floppy disk. £5.00 (inc p&p.)

Disk **16**. *Bishopwearmouth (1568-1837); Monkwearmouth (1583-1837).* 3½" floppy disk. £5.00 (inc. p&p.)

Disk **17**. *Sunderland (1719-1837); Whitburn (1579-1836).* 3½" floppy disk. £5.00 (inc. p&p.)

Northumberland

Disk **18**. *Blanchland (1753-1837); Bywell St. Andrew (1686-1837); Bywell St. Peter (1663-1846); Halton (1654-1769); Horton (1665-1837); Ovingham (1679-1837); Shotley (1670-1837); Slaley (1725-1837).* 3½" floppy disk. £5.00 (inc. p&p.)

Disk 19. *Hexham (1540-1837); Kirkhaugh (1761-1837); Knaresdale (1701-1837); Lambley (1743-1837).* 3½" floppy disk. £5.00 (inc. p&p.)

Disk 20. *Newburn (1659-1837); Newcastle St. Andrew (1589-1837.* 3½" floppy disk. £5.00 (inc. p&p.)

Oxford University Press

CWO Department, FREEPOST, NH 4051, Saxon Way West, Corby, Northamptonshire, NN18 9BR.

Phone: (01536) 741727

Email: ep.info@oup.co.uk

Webpage: www.oup.co.uk

Prices

Prices quoted are for individual users only. Please visit the web site for educational and commercial site licences

Bodleian Library pre-1920 catalogue of printed books. ISBN 0-19-268633-X. £195.00 + p&p £2.00 + V.A.T. Lists 1,300,000 books, many of genealogical interest.

Dictionary of national biography. ISBN: 0-19-268312-8. £150 + V.A.T. Originally published in 32 volumes, 1885-1900, with regular supplements subsequently.

Royal Historical Society bibliography on CD-Rom: the history of Britain, Ireland and the British overseas. ISBN: 0-19-268573-2. £250.00 + V.A.T. The authoritative listing of c.250,000 books and journal articles on British history - including many of genealogical relevance. Consolidates numerous printed bibliographies.

Who's who, 1897-1998. ISBN: 0-7136-4516-4. £250.00 + V.A.T. Includes the 9 volumes of *Who was who,* 1897-1995, *Who's who,* 1998, *etc.*

Phillimore

Shopwyke Manor Barn, Chichester, West Sussex, PO2 8BG.

Phone: (01243) 787636

Fax: (01243) 787639

Email: bookshop@phillimore.co.uk

Webpage: www.phillimore.co.uk

Great Domesday book on CD-Rom. £350.00. CD edition of the Phillimore translation of the 1086 Domesday book (which is also available in 40 hard copy vols.)

Powys Family History Society

c/o M.E. MacSorley, 112 Holbein Close, Basingstoke, Hants., RG21 3EX.

Breconshire 1851 census. £12.00 (inc. UK p&p). Contents: 'as enumerated' transcripts and full surname indexes.

Radnorshire 1841 census. £12.00 (inc. UK p&p). Contents: 'as enumerated' transcripts and full surname index.

Montgomeryshire 1851 census. £12.00 (inc. UK p&p). Contents: 'as enumerated' transcripts and full surname index.

Wills volume 1: the Diocese of St.David's. £12.00 (inc. UK p&p). Contents: 150 Wills, administrations and inventories, 1562-1850 mainly from Breconshire and Radnorshire, but including a few from Herefordshire and Monmouthshire.

Wills volume 2: the Diocese of St.David's. £12.00 (inc. UK p&p). Contents: 212 wills, administrations and inventories, 1612-1671, mainly from Breconshire and Radnorshire, but including a few from Herefordshire and Monmouthshire.

Quintin Publications

22 Delta Drive, Pawtucket, RI., 02860-4555, U.S.A.
Email: info@quintinpublications.com
Website: www.quintinpublications.com

The history of parish registers in England; also of the registers of Scotland, Ireland, the East and West Indies, the dissenters, and the episcopal chapels in and about London / John Southerden Burn. 2nd ed. originally published 1862. Ref. CD142. $US17.95.

A topographical dictionary of England / Samuel Lewis. 5th ed. Originally published in 4 vols. 1842. Ref. CD60. $US19.95.

Cary's new map of England and Wales with part of Scotland. Originally published 1794. Ref. CD11. $US29.95.

The place names of the Liverpool district / Henry Harrison. Originally published 1898. Ref. CD86. $US19.95.

The place names of Cumberland and Westmoreland / W. J. Sedgfield. Originally published 1915. Ref. CD118. $US19.95.

The place names of Buckinghamshire / A. Mawer & F. M. Stenton. Originally published 1925. Ref. CD105. $US19.95.

The place names of Surrey / A. Mawer & J. E. B. Gover, et al. Ref. CD104. Originally published 1934. $US19.95.

Cassell's gazetteer of Great Britain and Ireland. Originally published in 6 vols., 1900. Ref CD14. $US39.95.

The comprehensive gazetteer of England and Wales / J. H. F. Bradner. Ref. CD94. Originally published 1880. $US29.95.

Harleian Society Publications

The visitation of the County of Leicester in the year 1619 taken by William Camden, Clarenceaux King of arms / John Featherston (ed.) Originally published Harleian Society **2**. 1870. Ref. CD247. $US19.95.

The visitation of the County of Rutland in the year 1618-19 taken by William Camden, Clarenceaux King of arms, and other descents of families not in the visitation / George John Armytage (ed.) Originally published Harleian Society **3**. 1870. Ref. CD248. $US19.95.

The visitations of the County of Nottingham in the years 1569 and 1614 with many other descents of the same county / George William Marshall (ed.) Originally published Harleian Society **4**. 1871. Ref. CD249. $US19.95.

The visitations of the County of Oxford taken in the years 1566-1634 ... together with the gatherings of Oxfordshire collected by Richard Lee in 1574 / William Henry Turner (ed.) Originally published Harleian Society **5**. 1871. Ref. CD250. $US19.95.

Quintin Publications (*continued*)

The visitation of the County of Devon in the year 1620 / F. T. Colby (ed.) Originally published Harleian Society 6. 1872. Ref. CD251. $US19.95.

The visitation of the County of Cumberland in the year 1615, taken by Richard St. George, Norroy King of armes / John Fetherston (ed.) Originally published Harleian Society 7. 1872. Ref. CD252. $US19.95.

Le Nevé's pedigrees of the Knights made by King Charles II, King James II, King William III, and Queen Mary, King William alone, and Queen Anne / George W. Marshall (ed.) Originally published Harleian Society 8. Ref. CD253. $US20.95.

The visitation of the County of Cornwall in the year 1620 / J. L. Vivian & Henry H. Drake (eds.) Originally published Harleian Society 9. 1874. Ref. CD254. $US19.95.

The marriage, baptismal and burial registers of the Collegiate church or Abbey of St. Peter, Westminster / Joseph Lemuel Chester (ed.) Originally published Harleian Society 10. 1876. Ref. CD255. $US23.95.

The visitation of the County of Somerset in the year 1623 / Frederic Thomas Colby (ed.) Originally published Harleian Society 11. 1876. Ref. CD256. $US19.95.

The visitation of the County of Warwick in the year 1619, taken by William Camden, Clarenceaux King of arms / John Fetherston (ed.) Originally published Harleian Society 12. 1877. $US19.95.

The visitations of Essex by Hawley, 1552, Hervey 1558, Cooke, 1570, Raven 1612, and Owen and Lilly 1634, to which are added miscellaneous Essex pedigrees, from various Harleian manuscripts, and an appendix containing Berry's Essex pedigrees / Walter C. Metcalfe (ed.) Originally published Harleian Society 13-14. 1878-9. Ref. CD258. $US23.95.

The visitation of London, anno Domini 1633, 1634 and 1635, made by Sr. Henry St. George, Kt., Richmond herald, and deputy and marshall to Sr. Richard St. George, Clarencieux King of armes / Joseph Jackson Howard & Joseph Lemuel Chester (eds.) Originally published Harleian Society 15 & 17. 1880-83. $US23.95.

The visitation of Yorkshire in the years 1563 and 1564 made by William Flower / Charles Best Norcliffe (ed.) Originally published Harleian Society 16. 1881. Ref. CD260. $US19.95.

The visitation of Cheshire in the year 1580 made by Robert Glover, Somerset herald, for William Flower, Norroy King of arms with numerous additions and continuations including those from the visitation of Cheshire made in the year 1566 by the same herald, with an appendix containing the visitation of a part of Cheshire in the year 1533 made by William Fellows, Lancaster herald for Thomas Benolte, Clarenceaux King of arms. And a fragment of the visitation of the City of Chester in the year 1591 made by Thomas Chalmers, deputy to the office of Arms / John Paul Rylands (ed.) Originally published Harleian Society 18. 1882. Ref. CD261. $US19.95.

The visitations of Bedfordshire, annis domini 1566, 1582 and 1634, made by William Harvey, esq., Clarencieulx King of arms, Robert Cooke, esq. Clarencieulx King of arms, and George Owen, esq., York herald, as deputy for Sir Richard St. George, kt., Clarencieulx King of arms, together with additional pedigrees, chiefly from Harleian ms.1531, and an appendix, containing a list of pedigrees entered at the visitation of 1669; also lists of Bedfordshire Knights and gentry taken from Lansdowne ms.877 / Frederic Augustus Blaydes (ed.) Originally published Harleian Society **19**. 1884. Ref. CD261. $US19.95.

The visitation of the County of Dorset, taken in the year 1623 by Henry St. George, Richmond herald, and Sampson Lennard, bluemantle pursuivant, marshals and deputies to William Camden, Clarenceux King of arms / John Paul Rylands (ed.) Originally published Harleian Society **20**. 1885. $US19.95.

The visitation of the County of Gloucester taken in the year of 1623 by Henry Chitty and John Phillipot as deputies to William Camden, Clarenceux King of arms, with pedigrees from the herald's visitations of 1569 and 1582-3, and sundry miscellaneous pedigrees / Sir John Maclean & W. C. Heane (eds.) Originally published Harleian Society **21**. 1885. Ref. CD264. $US19.95.

The visitation of Herefordshire made by Robert Cooke, Clarencieux, in 1569 / Frederic William Weaver (ed.) Originally published Harleian Society **22**. 1886. Ref. CD265. $US19.95.

Allegations for marriage licences issued from the Dean and Chapter of Westminster 1558 to 1699. Ref. CD266. Originally published Harleian Society **23**. 1886. $US19.95.

Allegations for marriage licences issued from the Faculty Office of the Archbishop of Canterbury at London, 1543 to 1689, extracted by Joseph Lemuel Chester / Geo. J. Armytage (ed.) Originally published Harleian Society **24**. 1886. Ref. CD267. $US19.95.

Allegations for marriage licences issued by the Bishop of London 1528 to [1828], extracted by Joseph Lemuel Chester / Geo J. Armytage (ed.) Originally published Harleian Society **25-6**. 1887. Ref. CD268. $US23.95.

The visitation of the County of Worcester made in the year 1569, with other pedigrees relating to that county from Richard Mundy's collection / W. P. W. Phillimore (ed.) Originally published Harleian Society **27**. 1888. Ref. CD269. $US19.95.

The visitation of Shropshire taken in the year 1623 by Robert Tresswell, Somerset herald, and Augustine Vincent, Rouge croix pursuivant of arms, marshals and deputies to William Camden, Clarenceux King of arms, with additions from the pedigrees of Shropshire gentry taken by the heralds in the years 1569 and 1584 and other sources / George Grazebrook & John Paul Rylands (eds.) Originally published Harleian Society **28-9**. 1889. Ref. CD270. $US23.95.

Allegations for marriage licences issued by the vicar-general of the Archbishop of Canterbury / George J. Armytage. Originally published Harleian Society **30-31** & **33-4**. 1890-92. Ref. CD271. $US39.95.

The visitacion of Norffolk made and taken by William Harvey, Clarencieux King of arms, anno 1563, enlarged with another visitacion made by Clarenceux Cooke, with many other descents, and also the vissitation made by John Raven anno 1613 / Walter Rye (ed.) Originally published Harleian Society **32**. 1891. Ref. CD272. $US19.95.

Hampshire allegations for marriage licences granted by the Bishop of Winchester, 1689 to 1837 / William J. C. Moens (ed.) Originally published Harleian Society **35-6**. 1893. Ref. CD273 $US23.95.

Familiae minorum gentium, diligentia Josephi Hunter / John W. Clay (ed.) Originally published Harleian Society **37-40**. 1894-6. Ref. CD274. $US39.95.

The visitation of Cambridge made in a (1575), continued and enlarged with the vissitation of the county made by Henery St. George, Richmond herald, marshall and deputy to William Camden, Clarenceulx, in a 1619, with many other descents added therto / John W. Clay (ed.) Originally published Harleian Society **41**. 1897. Ref. CD275. $US19.95.

The visitation of Kent taken in the years 1619-1623 by John Philipot, rouge dragon, marshal and deputy to William Camden, Clarenceux / Robert Hovenden (ed.) Originally published Harleian Society **42**. 1898. Ref. CD276. $US19.95.

The visitations of the county of Surrey made and taken in the years 1530 by Thomas Benolte, Clarenceux King of arms, 1572 by Robert Cooke, Clarenceux King of arms and 1623 by Samuel Thompson, Windsor herald and Augustin Vincent, Rouge croix pursuivant, marshals and deputies to William Camden, Clarenceux King of arms / W. Bruce Bannerman (ed.) Originally published Harleian Society **43**. 1899. Ref. CD277. $US19.95.

Obituary prior to 1800 (as far as relates to England, Scotland and Ireland, com. Sir William Musgrave / Sir George J. Armytage (ed.) Originally published Harleian Society **44-9**. 1899-1901. Ref. CD278. $US39.95.

Lincolnshire pedigrees / A.R. Maddison (ed.) Originally published Harleian Society **50-52** & **55**. 1901-6. Ref. CD279. $US39.95.

The visitations of the County of Sussex made and taken in the years 1530 by Thomas Benolte, Clarenceux, King of arms, and 1633-4 by John Philipot, Somerset herald, and George Owen, York herald for Sir John Burroughs, Garter, and Sir Richard St. George, Clarenceux / W. Bruce Bannerman (ed.) Originally published Harleian Society **53**. 1905. Ref. CD280. $US19.95.

A visitation of the County of Kent, begun anno Dni. MDCLIII finished anno Dni MDCLXVIII / Sir George J. Armytage (ed.) Originally published Harleian Society **54**. 1906. Ref. CD281. $US19.95.

The four visitations of Berkshire made and taken by Thomas Benolte ... et al / W. Harry Rylands (ed.) Originally published Harleian Society **56-7**. 1907-8. $US25.95. Visitations of 1532, 1566, 1623, & 1665-6.

The visitation of the County of Buckingham made in 1634 by John Philipot esq., Somerset herald, and William Ryley, bluemantle pursuivant, marshals and deputies to Sir Richard St. George, Knight, Clarenceux, and Sir John Borough, Knight, Garter, who visited as Norroy by mutual agreement; including the church notes then taken. Together with pedigrees from the visitation made in 1566 by William Harvey esq., Clarenceux, and some pedigrees from other sources / W. Harry Rylands (ed.) Originally published Harleian Society **58**. 1909. $US19.95.

Pedigrees made at the visitation of Cheshire, 1613, taken by Richard St. George, esq., Norroy King of arms, and Henry St. George, gent, bluemantle pursuivant and arms; and some other contemporary pedigrees / Sir George J. Armytage. Originally published Harleian Society **59**. 1909. Ref. CD284. $US19.95.

A visitation of the County of Surrey, begun anno Dni MDCLXII, finished MDCLXVIII / Sir George Armytage, Bt. Originally published Harleian Society **60**. 1910. Ref. CD285. $US19.95.

A visitation of the County of Suffolk, begun anno Dni 1664 and finished anno Dni.1668 by Sir Edward Bysshe, Kt., Clarenceux, King of arms / W. Harry Rylands (ed.) Originally published Harleian Society **61**. 1910. Ref. CD286. $US19.95.

The visitation of the County of Warwick begun by Thomas May, Chester, and Gregory King, Rouge dragon, in Hilary vacac__n 1682, reviewed by them in the Trinity vacac__n following, and finished by Henry Dethick, Richmond, and the said rouge dragon pursuivant, in Trinity vacation 1683, by virtue of several deputations from Sir Henry St. George, Clarenceux, King of arms / W. Harry Rylands (ed.) Originally published Harleian Society **62**. 1911. Ref. CD287. $US19.95.

Staffordshire pedigrees based on the visitation of that county made by William Dugdale esquire, Norroy King of arms, in the years 1663-1664 / Sir George J. Armytage, Bart., & W. Harry Rylands (eds.) Originally published Harleian Society **63**. 1912. Ref. CD288. $US19.95.

Pedigrees from the visitation of Hampshire made by Thomas Benolte, Clarenceulx, a 1530, enlarged with the visitation of the same county made by Robert Cooke, Clarenceulx, anno 1575, both which are continued with the visitation made by John Phillipott, Somersett (for William Camden) in a 1634, as collected by Richard Mundy in Harleian ms. no.1544 / W. Harry Rylands (ed.) Originally published Harleian Society **64**. 1913. Ref. CD289. $US19.95.

Middlesex pedigrees as collected by Richard Mundy in Harleian ms. no.1551 / Sir George John Armytage (ed.) Originally published Harleian Society **65**. 1914. $US19.95.

Quintin Publications (*continued*)

Grantees of arms named in docquets and patents to the end of the seventeenth century, in the manuscripts preserved in the British Museum, the Bodleian Library, Oxford, Queens College, Oxford, Gonville and Caius College, Cambridge, and elsewhere, alphabetically arranged by the late Joseph Foster and contained in the Additional ms. no.37,147 in the British Museum / W. Harry Rylands (ed.) Originally published Harleian Society **66**. 1915. Ref. CD291. $US19.95.

Grantees of arms named in docquets and patents betwwen the years 1687 and 1898, preserved in various manuscripts, collected and alphabetically arranged by the late Joseph Foster and contained in the Additional ms. no. 37,149 in the British Museum / W. Harry Rylands (ed.) Originally published Harleian Society **67-8**. 1916-17. Ref. CD292. $US23.95.

Allegations for marriage licences in the Archdeaconry of Sudbury, in the County of Suffolk / W. Bruce Bannerman & G.G.Bruce Bannerman (eds). Originally published Harleian Society **69-72**. 1918-21. Ref. CD293. $US39.95.

The visitation of the County of Rutland, begun by Fran. Burghill, Somerset, and Gregory King, Rougedragon, on Trinity vacation 1681; carried on and finished by Tho. May, Chester herald, and the said Rougedragon pursuivant in Hillary and Trinity vacation 1682, by virtue of several deputacions from Sir Henry St. George, Kt., Clarenceux King of arms / W. Harry Rylands & W. Bruce Bannerman (eds). Originally published Harleian Society **73**. 1922.

Wales

Transactions of the West Wales Historical Society volume 1-14 (complete series). Ref. CD37. $US29.95. Many articles of genealogical interest.

A topographical dictionary of Wales / Samuel Lewis. 2nd ed. Originally published in 2 vols. 1842. Ref. CD57. $US19.95.

Handbook of the origin of place-names in Wales and Monmouthshire / Thomas Morgan. Originally published 1887. $US19.95.

Scotland

The history of the Celtic place-names of Scotland / William Watson. Originally published 1926. Ref. CD88. $US22.95.

The gazetteer of Scotland / John Wilson. Originally published 1882. Ref. CD52. $US19.95.

A topographical dictionary of Scotland / Samuel Lewis. Originally published in 4 vols., 1846. Ref. CD58. $US19.95.

Ireland

A topographical dictionary of Ireland / Samuel Lewis. Originally published in 2 vols, 1842. Ref. CD59. $US19.95.

Atlas and cyclopedia of Ireland. Originally published 1900. Ref. CD33. $US39.95.

Memorial atlas of Ireland showing provinces, counties, baronies, parishes etc. Ref. CD30. $US29.95.

The place names of County Wicklow / Liam Price. Originally published 1945. Ref. CD106. $US19.95.

Place names of the County of Longford / Joseph MacGivney. Originally published 1908. Ref. CD62. $US19.95.

Indexes to Irish wills / W.P.W. Phillimore. Originally
published in 5 vols. Ref. CD34. $US29.95. Covers wills
probated pre-1800 in many dioceses.

Journal of the American Irish Historical Society, 1898-1932. 32
vols. Ref. CD36. $US39.95. 5000+ pages of historical and
genealogical articles.

Royal Historical Society
See Oxford University Press

S & N Genealogy Supplies
Greenacres, Salisbury Road, Chilmark, Salisbury. SP3 5AH.
Phone: (01722) 716121
Email: Genealogy Supplies@compuserve.com
Webpage: www.genealogy.demon.co.uk

1891 census Project: London. Cds forthcoming for North East
London, South West London North West London, & South
East London. £24.95 per region, or £69.00 the set. This
project will eventually cover the whole country.

Interactive UK research guide. £5.95. Includes *How to
research your family history,* with web links and lists of
institutions.

Value of the pound (1600 to 1996). £8.75. Calculates the
current value of money from the sums mentioned in your
documents.

British date calculator (years covered 1,000 to 2,050). £8.75.

Army search. 3½" floppy disk. £6.95. Finding aid for army
ancestors.

Begin search. 3½" floppy disk. £6.95. Finding aid.

Complete guide to heraldry. £19.95.

UK 1851 census extract data. £29.95. Extracts 500,000 names,
i.e. 2 of the full census

Names: an index to changes of name / W.P.W. Phillimore.
Originally published 1905. £24.95.

Maps: England & Wales 1897 Bartholomew's Royal atlas.
£19.95.

Burke's peerage 1885. £29.95.

*Landowner's in Scotland 1872: owners of one acre or more in
1872/73.* £24.95.

Peerage CD 26 / John Bloore. £29.95. Gedcom database with
100,000 entries for peers of the realm and their
descendents.

*Kelly's directory of the landed gentry and official classes
19006.* £29.95.

Tri-county CD of Devon, Norfolk, and Warwick. £9.95.
Photographs of churches, maps, *etc.*

UK deeds index database. £9.95.

CD Atlas of various maps for the UK from 1800-1900. £19.95.
Forthcoming.

Bartholomew's 1898 atlas. 2 CDs. £19.95.

Bedfordshire
Bedfordshire 1823 Pigot's directory. £19.95.

S & N Genealogy Supplies (*continued*)

Berkshire

Berkshire Phillimore parish records (marriages). Originally published 1908-14. 2 CDs. £19.95 per CD. Contents:
- Vol.1. Wantage & West Woodhay. £19.95.
- Vol.2. Bradfield, Buscot, Harwell, Kingston Lyell, Purley, Sparsholt, Sulham, West Hannay, & West Hendred. £19.95.

Berkshire. Bisham baptisms, marriages and burials 1560-1812. Originally published Parish Register Society **15**. 1898. £19.95.

Berkshire. Upton baptisms, marriages and burials 1588-1741. Originally published Parish Register Society **8**. 1907. £19.95.

Buckinghamshire

Buckinghamshire Phillimore parish records (marriages). Originally published 1902-23. 9 CD's. £19.95 per CD. Or £89.77 for all vols. on one CD. Forthcoming. Contents:
- Vol.1. Cheddington, Cholesbury, Edlesborough, Hawridge, Masworth, Mentmore, Pitstone, Slapton, Soulbury.
- Vol.2. Wendover, Ivinghoe, Aston Clinton, Hormead.
- Vol.3. Wing, Grove, Stone, Hartwell, Linslade, Drayton Parslow, Aston Clinton (St. Leonard's), Sherington, Westbury, Chicheley.
- Vol.4. Amersham, Chenies, Chalfont St. Giles, Chalfont St. Peter, Hedgerley, Stoke Poges.
- Vol.5. Beaconsfield, Burnham, Wooburn, Hedsor, Hitcham, Taplow, Dorney, Fulmer.
- Vol.6. High Wycombe, Bradenham, Fingest, Ibstone, Turville.
- Vol.7. Hughendon, Little Missenden, Denham.
- Vol.8. Iver, Chesham.
- Vol.9. Newport Pagnell, Lathbury, Broughton, Moulsoe.

Buckinghamshire 1823 Pigot's directory. £19.95.
Buckinghamshire 1844 Pigot's directory. £19.95.

Cambridgeshire

Cambridgeshire Phillimore parish records (marriages). Originally published 1907-27. 8 CD's. £19.95 per CD. Or £79.30 for all vols. on 1 CD. Forthcoming.
- Vol.1. Cambridge (St.Edwards), Fen Drayton, Knapwell.
- Vol.2. Cambridge (St.Sepulchre's), Conington, Swavesey, Over, Lolworth.
- Vol.3. Boxworth, Long Stanton (All Saints), Long Stanton (St.Michael), Oakington, Girton, Dry Drayton, Cambridge (St.Botolph's), Modingley, Toft, Caldecot.
- Vol.4. Cambridge (All Saints), Croxton, Eltisley, Elsworth, Graveley, Papworth St.Agnes, Papworth Everard.
- Vol.5. Cambridge (St.Andrew the Great), Histon, Impington, Cambridge (St.Peter).
- Vol.6. Cambridge (St.Giles), Milton, Willingham.
- Vol.7. Cambridge (St.Andrew the Less), Cambridge (St.Benedict), Chesterton, Cambridge (St.Edward).
- Vol.8. Cambridge (St.Mary the Great), Cambridge (St.Mary the Less), Cambridge (St.Clement).

Cheshire

Cheshire Phillimore parish records (marriages). Originally published 1909-14. 5 CD's. £19.95 per CD. Or £49.35 for all vols. on 1 CD. Forthcoming. Contents:

Vol.1. Disley, Marple, Taxal, Lymm, Christleton, Gawsworth. £19.95.

Vols.2-4. Prestbury. 3 CDs; £19.95 each.

Vol.5. Alderley, Bosley, Capesthorne, Chelford, Marton, Poynton cum Worth, Siddington, Pott Shrigley, Taxal, Marton. £19.95.

Cheshire. Upton in Overchurch 1600-1812 baptisms, marriages and burials. Originally published Parish Register Society **33**. 1900. £19.95. Forthcoming.

Cheshire 1855 Slater' directory. £19.95.

Cornwall

Cornwall Phillimore parish records (marriages). Originally published 1900-35. 26 CD's. £19.95 per CD. All 26 vols. on 1 CD, £259.35. Contents:

Vol.1. Advent 1675-1812; Davidstow 1676-1812; Forrabury 1676-1812; Lanteglos by Camelford 1558-1812; Lesnewth 1569-1812; Michaelstow 1539-1812; Minster 1676-1812; Otterham 1687-1812; St.Breward 1558-1812; St.Clether 1640-1812; St.Juliot 1656-1812; St.Teath 1558-1812; Trevalga 1539-1812. £19.95.

Vol.2. Egloskerry 1574-1812; Laneast 1680-1812; Lanivet 1608-1812; Phillack 1572-1812; St.Mabyn 1562-1812; St.Tudy 1560-1812; Tintagel 1588-1812; Tremaine 1674-1812. £19.95.

Vol.3. Gwithian 1560-1812; St.Buryan 1654-1812; St.Just in Penwith 1599-1812; St.Levan 1694-1812; St.Sennen 1676-1812; Towednack 1676-1812. £19.95.

Vol.4. Blisland 1539-1812; Cardynham 1675-1812; Endellion 1684-1812; Helland 1677-1812; Lanhydrock 1559-1812; Sheviock 1570-1812; St.Merryn 1689-1812; St.Minver 1559-1812; Warleggan 1682-1812. £19.95.

Vol.5. Ludgvan 1563-1812; Sancreed 1559-1812; St.Breage 1559-1812; St.Germoe 1674-1812. £19.95.

Vol.6. Egloshayle 1600-1812; Padstow 1599-1812; St.Kew 1564-1812; St.Sampson (Golant) 1568-1812; Warleggan 1547-1718; Withiel 1568-1812;£19.95.

Vol.7. Manaccan 1633-1812; Mawnan 1553-1812; Mylor 1673-1812; Perranarworthal 1684-1812; St.Sithney 1654-1812; Stythians 1654-1812. £19.95.

Vol.8. Fowey 1568-1812; Lostwithiel 1609-1812; Luxulyan 1594-1812; St.Cleer 1678-1812; Tywardreath 1642-1812. £19.95.

Vol.9. Lelant 1679-1812; Paul 1595-1812; St.Hilary 1676-1812; Zennor 1617-1812. £19.95.

Vol.10. Lanlivery 1600-1812; Menheniot 1554-1812; St.Ewe 1560-1812; St.Stephen in Brannel 1681-1812; St.Winnow 1622-1812. £19.95.

Vol.11; Bodmin 1559-1812; Lezant 1539-1812; St.Gorran 1668-1812; St.Wenn 1678-1812. £19.95.

Vol.12. Gulval 1686-1741; Gwinear 1560-1812; Madron 1674-1812; Morvah (see Madron post 1722) 1617-1722. £19.95.

Vol.13. Budock 1653-1812; St.Colan 1665-1812; St.Gluvias 1599-1812. £19.95.

Vol.14; Lewannick 1675-1812; St.Columb Minor 1560-1812; St.Issey 1596-1812; St.Ives 1653-1812; St.Mawgan in Meneage 1563-1812. £19.95.

Vol.15; Constantine 1571-1812; Perranuthnoe 1589-1812; St.Martin in Meneage 1563-1812; Wendron 1560-1812. £19.95.

Vol. 16. Lanherne Convent RC 1710-1834; Little Petherick (St.Petrock Minor); Perranzabuloe 1619-1812; St.Columb Major 1781-1812; St.Crantock 1559-1812; St.Cubert 1608-1812; St.Ervan 1602-1812; St.Eval 1631-1812; St.Mawgan in Pydar 1608-1812; St.Newlyn in Pydar 1559-1812; St.Petrock Minor 1636-1812. £19.95.

Vol.17; Boyton 1568-1812; Linkinhorne 1576-1812; Morwinstow 1558-1812; Pillaton 1557-1812; Roche 1578-1812; South Petherwin 1656-1812; St.Mellion 1558-1812. £19.95.

Vol. 18; Crowan 1674-1812; St.Agnes 1596-1812; St.Allen 1611-1812; St.Breock 1561-1812. £19.95.

Vol. 19. Boyton II 1754-1812; Camborne 1538-1812; Redruth 1614-1812. £19.95.

Vol.20; Botus Fleming 1550-1812; Kilkhampton 1539-1812; Poughill 1537-1812; St.Anthony in Meneage 1726-1812; St.Enoder 1571-1812; St.Erme 1614-1812; St.Erth 1563-1812. £19.95.

Vol.21; Helston 1599-1812; Landrake 1583-1812; Landulph 1541-1812; St.Dennis 1610-1812; St.Erney 1555-1812; Stratton 1674-1812. £19.95.

Vol.22. Kea 1653-1812; Kenwyn 1559-1812; Tregony 1661-1812. £19.95.

Vol.23. Cornelly 1679-1812; Ladock 1686-1812; Launcells 1642-1812; Marhamchurch 1558-1812; Probus 1641-1812; St.Stephen by Launceston 1566-1812; St.Veryan 1676-1812. £19.95.

Vol.24. Launceston 1559-1812; St.Keverne 1608-1812. £19.95.

Vol.25. Grade 1708-1812; Gwennap 1660-1812; Jacobstow 1656-1812; Landewednack 1654-1812; Poundstock 1615-1812; Ruan Major 1683-1812; Ruan Minor 1667-1812; Treneglos 1694-1812; Warbstow 1695-1812; Week St.Mary 1602-1812. £19.95.

Vol.26. Creed (with Grampound) 1611-1837; Gerrans 1538-1837; Philleigh 1613-1837; Ruan Lanyhorne 1608-1837; St.Clement 1538-1837; St.Just in Roseland 1538-1812; St.Michael Penkivel 1577-1837. Devon vol.l. Werrington 1654-1812. £19.95.

Cornwall 1823 and 1844 Pigot's directory. £19.95.

Cornwall 1893 Kelly's directory. £19.95.

Cumberland
Cumberland 1855 Slater's directory. £19.95.

Derbyshire
Derbyshire Phillimore parish records (marriages). Originally published 1906- . 15 CD's. £19.95 per CD. Or all 15 vols. on 1 CD, £149.62. Contents:

Vol.1. Boulton 1756-1812; Breaston 1719-1810; Church Broughton 1538-1812; Dale Abbey 1667-1813; Hault Hucknall 1660-1812; Heath *alias* Lownd or Lund 1682-1812; Mackworth 1603-1812; Ockbrook 1631-1812; Risley 1720-1812; Sandiacre 1581-1812; Stanley 1754-1812; Stanton by Dale 1605-1812. £19.95.

Vol.2. Brailsford 1653-1812; Duffield 1598-1766. £19.95.

Vol.3. Duffield 1766-1812; Kirk Ireton 1572-1812; Mellor 1678-1775; Spondon 1658-1812. £19.95.

Vol.4. Derby St.Alkmunds 1538-1812; Foremark 1663-1812; Quarndon 1755-1812; Tickenhall 1628-1812. £19.95

Vol. 5. Chaddesden 1718-1812; Morton 1575-1812; Norton 1559-1812; Derby St. Michaels, 1559-1812; West Hallam 1638-1812. £19.95.

Vol. 6. Alvaston 1614-1812; Chellaston 1570-1812; Derby St.Peters 1558-1812; Kirk Langley 1654-1812; Normanton by Derby 1769-1810; Osmaston by Derby 1743-1812; Willington 1698-1812. £19.95.

Vol. 7. Horsley 1558-1812; Ilkeston 1588-1812; Kirk Hallam 1700-1837; Matlock 1637-1812. £19.95.

Vol. 8. Alsop en le Dale 1701-1837; Aston upon Trent 1667-1812; Barrow on Trent & Twyford 1657-1812; Ilkeston 1785-1791; Melbourne 1653-1812; Parwich 1639-1837; Smisby 1720-1812; Stanton by Bridge 1664-1837; Swarkeston 1604-1837; Weston upon Trent 1565-1812. £19.95.

Vol. 9. Derby. All Saints 1558-1837. £19.95.

Vol. 10. Derby St. Werburgh 1558-1837. £19.95

Vol. 11. Beauchief 1560-1837; Beighton 1653-1837; Dronfield 1696-1837. £19.95.

Vol.12. Buxton 1718-1837; Chapel-en-le-Frith 1621-1837; Fairfield 1756-1837; Repton 1578-1837. £19.95.

Vol.13. Breadsall 1573-1837; Elvaston 1651-1837; Kedleston 1600-1837; Morley 1540-1837; Sawley 1656-1837; Smalley 1624-1837; Wilne 1540-1837. £19.95

Vol. 14. Denby 1577-1834; Elwall 1557-1837; Longford 1539-1837; Pentrich 1640-1837; Pentrich protestation roll 1641; Shirland 1695-1837; Stanley 1754-1837; South Wingfield 1585-1837; South Wingfield protestation 1641. £19.95.

Vol.15. Heanor 1558-1837. £19.95.

Devon

Devonshire Phillimore parish records (marriages). Originally published 1909-15. 2 CDs. Contents:

Vol.1. Countisbury, Ipplepen, Kingskerswell, Martinhoe, Trentishoe, Uffculme, and Werrington. £19.95.

Vol.2. Plymouth St. Andrew. £19.95.

Devon. Clyst St. George baptisms, marriages and burials 1565-1812. Originally published Parish Register Society **25**. 1899. £19.95.

Devonshire 1823 Pigot's directory. £19.95.

Devonshire 1844 Pigot's directory. £19.95.

Devonshire 1873 Kelly's directory. £19.95.

Dorset

Dorset. Beer Hackett baptisms, marriages and burials 1559-1812. Originally published Parish Register Society **3**. 1896.

Dorset. Lydlinch baptisms, marriages and burials 1559-1812. Originally published Parish Register Society **17**. 1899. £19.95.

Dorset. Tarrant Hinton baptisms, marriages and burials 1545-1812. Originally published Parish Register Society **44**. 1902. £19.95.

S & N Genealogy Supplies (*continued*)

Dorset Phillimore parish records (marriages). Originally published 1906-14. 7 CD's. £19.95 per CD. Or all 7 vols. on 1 CD £69.82. Contents:

Vol. 1. Powerstock & West Milton, Milton Abbey, Beaminster, Mapperton, Cattistock, Bothenhampton, Walditch, Bradpole, North Poorton, Chilfrome. £19.95.

Vol. 2. Charminster, Hook, Symondsbury, Chideock, Hawkchurch, Allington, Thorncombe, North Poorton. £19.95.

Vol. 3. Beaminster, Lyme Regis, Broadwinsor, Great Toller, Halstock, Frome Vauchurch, Wraxall, Cerne Abbas, Up Cerne. £19.95.

Vol. 4. Litton Cheney, Burstock, Charmouth, Stalbridge, Loders, Maiden Newton, South Perrot & Mosterton, Fordington St. George, West Chelborough. £19.95.

Vol. 5. Burton Bradstock with Shipton Gorge, Cheddington, Pilsdon, East Chelborough, Whitchurch Canonicorum, Marshwood, Wyke Regis. £19.95.

Vol. 6. Preston cum Sutton Poyntz, Wotton Fitzpaine, Corscombe, Godmanstone, Nether Cerne, Stoke Abbot, Swyre, Rampisham, Askerswell, Alton Pancras, Fleet, Langton Herring, East Stour. £19.95.

Vol. 7. Dorchester (Holy Trinity), Chickerell, Piddletown, Netherbury, Marshwood. £19.95.

Dorsetshire 1823 and 1844. Pigot's directory. £19.95.

Co.Durham

Durham. Lanchester All Saints 1560-1603. Memorials to 1608. Originally published 1909. £19.95.

Essex

Essex Phillimore parish records (marriages). Originally published 1909-14. 4 CD's. £19.95 per CD. Forthcoming. Contents:

Vol. 1. Boxted, Great Horkesley, Little Horkesley, Wormingford, Ashdon, Navestock. £19.95.

Vol. 2. Chelmsford. £19.95.

Vol. 3. Chelmsford (cont.), Writtle, Widford. £19.95.

Vol. 4. Walthamstow, Roxwell, Great Leighs, Little Leighs. £19.95.

Essex 1823 Pigot's directory. £5.95.

Gloucestershire

Gloucestershire Phillimore parish records (marriages). Originally published 1896-1914. 17 CD's. £19.95 per CD. Or all vols. on 1 CD. £169.58. Contents:

Vol.1. Kings Stanley, Owlpen, Quedgeley, Rendcombe, Swindon, Forthampton, Nimpsfield, & Slimbridge. £19.95.

Vol.2. Leonard Stanley, Stonehouse, Stinchcombe, Uley, and Chedworth. £19.95.

Vol.3. Aston Subedge, Bishop's Cleeve, Charlton King's, Dorsington, Nether Swell, Matson, Mickleton, and Stone. £19.95.

Vol.4. Hinton on the Green, Aston Somerville, Kemerton, Lemington Parva, Weston Avon, Buckland, Saintbury, Preston upon Stour, Stanton, Snowshill, Temple Guiting, Wormington, Childswickham, Weston Subedge, Guiting Power, Sutton under Brailes, Todenham. £19.95.

Vol.5. Coaley, Clifford Chambers, Dursley, Hawkesbury, and Moreton-in-the-Marsh. £19.95.

Vol.6. Batsford, Beverston, Ebrington, Elkstone, Standish, Stinchcombe, Weston Birt, Willersey, and Quinton. £19.95.

Vol.7. Cheltenham, Frampton-on-Severn, and Newington Bagpath. £19.95.

Vol.8. Painswick, Kingscote, and Cam. £19.95.

Vol.9. Winchcombe, Shipton Moyne, Old Sodbury, Kingswood, and Michel Dean. £19.95.

Vol.10. Avening, Alderley, Harescombe, Hill, Marston Sicca, and Tetbury. £19.95.

Vol.11. Minchinhampton, Wickwar, Slimbridge, Chipping Sodbury, Oldbury-on-the-Hill, and Didmarton. £19.95.

Vol.12. Horsley, Hardwicke, Cherrington, Ozleworth, Nimpsfield, Newington Bagpath, Tortworth, Edgworth, Syde, Duntisbourne Abbots, Coln Rogers. £19.95.

Vol.13. Horton, Boxwell, & Leighterton, Great Badminton, Twining, Filton, Wyck Risington, Acton Turville, Tormarton & W.Littleton, Eastington, Whaddon, Brookthorpe, Southrop, and Icombe. £19.95.

Vol.14. Frocester, Maismore, Tirley, Broadwell, Olveston, Woolastone, Alvington, Ashchurch, Westcote, and Turkdean. £19.95.

Vol.15. Thornbury, Oldbury-on-Severn, Naunton, Ampney Crucis, Sevenhampton, and Prestbury. £19.95.

Vol.16. Fairford, Henbury, Huntley, and Winstone. £19.95.

Vol.17. Bromesberrow, Minsterworth, Hatherop, Cold Aston, Duntisbourne Rous, Great Rissington, Bourton-on-the-Water, Lower Slaughter, Upper Slaughter, and Little Rissington. £19.95.

Gloucestershire. Bitton baptisms, marriages and burials 1572-1674. Originally published Parish Register Society **32**. 1900.

Gloucestershire 1844 Pigot's directory. £19.95.

Hampshire

Hampshire 1823 Pigot's directory. £5.95.

Hampshire Phillimore parish records (marriages). 16 CD's; £19.95 per CD. Or all 16 vols. on 1 CD, £159.60. Contents:

Vol.1. Bramley, Bullington, Cliddesden, Deane, Hurstbourne Priors, Hurstbourne Tarrant, Knight's Enham, Monxton, Penton Mewsey, St.Mary Bourne, Steventon, Tufton & Wooton St.Lawrence. £19.95.

Vol.2. Faccombe, Tangley, Coombe, Vernham, Yateley, Overton, Winslade, Aldershot, Up-Nately & Amport. £19.95.

Vol.3. Sherbourne St.John, Eversley, North Waltham, Church Oakley, Winchfield, Elvetham, Basing, Dogmersfield, Farnborough & Hartley Wintney. £19.95.

Vol.4. Winchester Cathedral, St.Swithun-Upon-Kingsgate Winchester & Crondall. £19.95.

Vol.5. Long Sutton, Strathfieldsaye, St.Michael Winchester, St.Lawrence Winchester, Basingstoke, Baughurst, Eastrop & Worting. £19.95.

Vol.6. Odiham, South Warnborough, Tadley, Heckfield & Stratfield Turgis. £19.95.

S & N Genealogy Supplies (*continued*)

Vol.7. Eling, Sopley, West Meon & Silchester. £19.95.

Vol.8. Highclere, Burghclere, Ewhurst, Wolverton, Rowner, Newtown, Litchfield, Newnham, Herriard, Tufton, & Whitchurch. £19.95.

Vol.9. East Woodhay, Sherfield upon Loddon, Hartley Westpall, Linkenholt, Laverstoke, Wonston, Bentley, Preston Candover & Popham. £19.95.

Vol.10. Portsmouth, St.Thomas £19.95.

Vol.11. Winchester College, Weyhill, Hannington, Crawley, Nateley Scures, Kingsworth, Bentworth, Rotheswick & Boldre. £19.95.

Vol.12. Brading, Calbourne, Freshwater, Niton, Whitwell. & Yaverland. £19.95.

Vol.13. Winchester, St.Maurice. £19.95.

Vol.14. Newport, Isle of Wight. £19.95.

Vol.15. St.Thomas a Becket, Portsmouth 1701-1775.

Vol.16. Winchester St.Thomas with St.Clement, St.Peter Cheesehill, St.Faith, St.Bartholomew, Hyde. £19.95.

Hampshire 1844 Pigot's directory. £19.95.

Herefordshire

Herefordshire Pigot's directory 1844. £19.95.

Hereford. Munsley baptisms, marriages and burials 1662-1812. Originally published Parish Register Society **46**. 1903. £19.95. Forthcoming.

Hertfordshire

Hertfordshire 1823 Pigot's directory. £5.95.

Hertfordshire Phillimore parish records (marriages). Originally published in 3 vols., 1907- . 3 CD's. Forthcoming. Contents:

Vol. 1. Great Berkhamstead, Barley, Kensworth, Letchworth, Aldbury, Offley, Eastwick. £19.95.

Vol. 2. Ardeley *als* Yardley, Berrington, Watton, Graveley cum Chesfield, Datchworth, Shephall, Walkern, Knebworth. £19.95.

Vol. 3. Rickmansworth, Bushey, Elstree, Gilston, Little Berkhamsted. £19.95.

Huntingdonshire

Huntingdonshire Phillimore parish records (marriages) vol.1. Originally published 1912. Forthcoming. £19.95. Contents: Ramsey, Little Raveley, Bury, Wistow.

Kent

Kent Phillimore parish records (marriages). 2 CDs. Originally published 1910. Contents:

Vol. 1. Penshurst, Eynsford, Charlton in Dover, Westerham, Lamberhurst. £19.95.

Vol. 2. Halstead, West Farleigh, Willesborough, Newington, Staplehurst, Wichling. £19.95.

Kent 1823 Pigot's directory. £5.95.

Lancashire

Lancashire. Burnley parish registers 1562-1653. Originally published Lancashire Parish Register Society 2. 1899. £19.95.

Lancashire. Bury parish registers. 1590-1616. Originally
published Lancashire Parish Register Society 1. 1898.
£19.95.

Lancashire. Bury parish registers 1617-1646. Originally
published Lancashire Parish Register Society 10. 1901.
£19.95.

Lancashire. Bury parish registers 1647-1698. Originally
published Lancashire Parish Register Society 24. 1905.
£19.95.

Lancashire. Chipping, 1559-1694. Originally published
Lancashire Parish Register Society 14. 1903. £19.95.

Lancashire. Colne parish registers 1559-1653. Originally
published Lancashire Parish Register Society 17. 1904.
£19.95.

Lancashire. Croston marriages and burials 1690-1727.
Originally published Lancashire Parish Register Society 20.
1904. £19.95.

*Lancashire. Croston bapt., marriages and burials 1538-1685;
bapt. 1690-1727.* Originally published Lancashire Parish
Register Society 6. 1900. £19.95

Lancashire. Didsbury St. James 1561-1757. Pt.1. Originally
published Lancashire Parish Register Society 8. 1900.
£19.95.

Lancashire. Didsbury St. James 1561-1757. Pt.2. Originally
published Lancashire Parish Register Society 9. 1901. £19.95.

Lancashire. Padiham 1573-1653. Originally published
Lancashire Parish Register Society 16. 1903. £19.95.

Lancashire. Wigan baptisms, marriages and burials 1580-1625.
Originally published Lancashire Parish Register Society 4.
1899. £19.95.

Lancashire. Wittington St. Michael parish register 1538-1764.
Originally published Lancashire Parish Register Society 3.
£19.95.

Lancashire 1855 Slater's directory. £19.95.

Leicestershire

Leicestershire Phillimore parish records (marriages).
Originally published in 12 vols., 1908- . 12 CDs. £19.95 per
CD. Or all 12 vols. on 1 CD, £119.70. Forthcoming. Contents:
Vol.1. Bottesford, Muston, Twyford cum Thorpe Satchville,
Coston, Scraptoft, Sibson, Congerston, Ratby, Gaddesby,
Scalford, Evington, Rotherby, Hoby, Frisby-on-the-
Wreak, Ragdale, Brooksby, Thrussington, Barkby,
Somerby, Kirby Bellars, Harston, Branston, Eaton,
Stathern, Harby, Hose, Redmile. £19.95.
Vol.2. Ab Kettleby cum Holwell, Scalford, Evington,
Rotherby, Hoby, Frisby-on-the-Wreak, Ragdale,
Brooksby, Thrussington, Barkby, Somerby Kirby Bellars.
Vol.3. Melton Mowbray, Burton Lazars, Freeby, Great Dalby,
Little Dalby.
Vol.4. Barkston, Plungar, Knipton, Croxton Kerrial, Harston,
Branston, Eaton, Stathern, Harby, Hose, Redmile.
Vol.5. Pickwell, Frolesworth, Leire, Ashby Parva, Sharnford,
Gilmorton, Burrough on the Hill, Bitteswell, Calthorpes.
Protestation oaths for Aylestone, Bitteswell, Frolesworth
& Gaddesby. £19.95.

S & N Genealogy Supplies (*continued*)

Vol.6. Ashby Folville, South Croxton, Hungerton, Beeby, Queniborough, Eastwell, Wartnaby, Grimston, Cossington, Ratcliffe on the Wreak, Seagrave, Syston, Withcote, Wymeswold, Sileby, Rearsby, Prestwold, Hoton, Wanlip, Swithland, Humberstone. £19.95.

Vol.7. Rothley, Keyham, Wykeham cum Caldwell, Barrow on Soar, Mountsorrell. £19.95.

Vol.8. Owston cum Newbold Saucey, Withcote, Wymeswold, Sileby, Rearsby, Prestwold, Hoton. £19.95.

Vol.9. Walton on the Wolds, Quorndon, Woodhouse, Wanlip, Swithland, Humberstone. £19.95.

Vol.10. Thurcaston cum Cropston, Belgrave, Birstall, Thurmaston, Thurnby, cum Bushby, Stoughton, Houghton on the Hill, Lowesby with Cold Newton, Tilton on the Hill. £19.95.

Vol.11. Goadby Marwood, Long Clawson, Old Dalby, Nether Broughton, Saxelbye (with Sholeby), Asfordby, Thorpe Arnold (with Brentingby) Wyfordby, Saxby, Stapleford. £19.95.

Vol.12. Aylestone (with Glen Parva, & Lubbesthorpe), Blaby, Glenfield, Braunston, Kirby Muxloe, Knighton, Wigston Magna. £19.95.

Lincolnshire

Lincolnshire Phillimore parish records (marriages). Originally published in 11 vols., 1905-21. 11 CD's. £19.95. Or all 11 vols. on 1 CD, £109.72. Forthcoming. Contents:

Vol.1. Spalding. £19.95.

Vol.2. West Allington, East Allington, Sedgebrook, Pinchbeck, Fleet. £19.95.

Vol.3. Surfleet, Swinderby, Norton Disney, North Scarle, South Kelsey (St. Mary), South Kelsey (St. Nicholas), Thurlby, Aubourn, South Hykeham, North Hykeham, Haddington, Skinnand. £19.95.

Vol.4. Eagle, Doddington Pigot, Skellingthorpe, Bassingham, Thorpe on the Hill, Heckington, Carlton le Moorland, Stapleford. £19.95.

Vol.5. Weston St. Mary, Cowbitt, Moulton. £19.95.

Vol.6. Long Bennington, Foston, Westborough cum Doddington, Claypole, Stubton. £19.95.

Vol.7. Alford, Rigsby with Ailby, Beesby, Hannah with Hagnaby, Markby, Maltby, Saleby with Thoresthorpe, Strubby with Woodthorpe, Sutton le Marsh. £19.95.

Vol.8. Boultham, Bracebridge, Waddington, Harmston, Boothby Graffoe, Navenby, Wellingore. £19.95.

Vol.9. Withern, Trusthorpe, Huttoft, Mablethorpe, Mumby, Mumby Chapel, Willoughby. £19.95.

Vol.10. Addlethorpe, Anderby, Bilsby with Asserby, & Thurlby, Claxby, Cumberworth, Farlesthorpe, Hogsthorpe, Ingoldmells, Well with Dexthorpe. £19.95.

Vol.11. Woolsthorpe, Denton, Harlaxton, Barrowby, Great Goreby, Somerby.

Lincolnshire with Port of Hull 1885 directory. £19.95.

Lincs. Coleby 1561-1812. Originally published Parish Register Society **48**. 1903. £19.95. Forthcoming.

Lincs. Doddington-Pigot baptisms, marriages, burials and inscriptions 1562-1812. Originally published Parish Register Society 14. 1898. £19.95. Forthcoming.

London
London 1823 Pigot's directory. £19.95.

London marriages and registers. Including all the London registers listed separately below, on 1 CD, £99.75.

London Phillimore parish records (marriages). Vols.1-[4]. St. James, Duke Place. Originally published 1900-02. 4 CD's. £19.95 per CD.

London registers: St. Dionis Backchurch. 1538-1745. Originally published Harleian Society: registers 3. 1878. £19.95.

London registers: St. Peter's, Cornhill. Pt.1. 1538-1666. Originally published Harleian Society: registers 1. 1877. £19.95.

London registers: St. Peter's, Cornhill. Pt. 2. 1667-1774. Originally published Harleian Society registers 4. 1879. £19.95.

London registers: Knightsbridge Holy Trinity 1658-1681. Originally published [1925]. £19.95.

London registers: Westminster Abbey / Collegiate Church 1655-1875. Originally published Harleian Society 10. 1875. £19.95.

London marriage licences, 1521-1869. Originally published 1887. £19.95.

Middlesex
Middlesex Phillimore parish records (marriages). 7 CD's. £19.95 per CD. Or all 7 vols on 1 CD, £69.82. Forthcoming. Contents:
Vol. 1. Acton, Heston, Hanwell, Harlington, Greenford. £19.95.
Vol. 2. Hillingdon, Hayes, Northolt, Ickenham, Cowley, West Drayton. £19.95.
Vol. 3. Hampton, Twickenham, Teddington. £19.95.
Vol. 4. New Brentford, Hounslow, Stanwell, Sunbury, Ashford, Feltham, Hanworth, Pinner. £19.95.
Vol. 5. Uxbridge, Harefield, Great Stanmore, Enfield. £19.95.
Vol. 6. Edmonton. £19.95.
Vol. 7. Finchley, South Mimms, Monken Hadley. £19.95.

Monmouthshire
Monmouthshire 1844 Pigot's directory. £19.95.

Norfolk
Norfolk Phillimore parish records (marriages). 12 CD's. £19.95 per CD. Or all 12 vols. on 1 CD, £119.70. Contents:
Vol.1. Acle, Hemblington, Brundall, Burlington, Upton, Witton by Blofield, Braydeston, Strumpshaw, Calthorpe, Ingworth, Southacre, East Lexham, Castleacre, Langley, and Narborough. £19.95.
Vol.2. Babingly, Bawsey, Chadgrave, Dunham Magna, Heacham, Holkham, Litcham, Wolferton, Narford, Sandringham, and Snettisham. £19.95.
Vol.3. Booton, Great Cressingham, Horstead, Langham Episcopi, Mundesley, Norwich St Mary Coslany, Ranworth, West Beckham, Panxworth. £19.95.

Vol.4. Barton Turf, Bedingham, Burnham Sutton, Carleton Rode, Gresham, Hedenham, Hickling, Ulph, Weeting, Weasenham St Mary, Weasenham All Saints. £19.95.

Vol.5. Castleacre, Cringleford, Ditchingham, Fring, Holme by the Sea, Holme Hale, Mautby, Runham, Herringby, Thrigby, Thwaite St Mary, Topcroft, West Newton and Woodton. £19.95.

Vol.6. East Barsham, Fakenham, North Barsham, Sculthorpe, Snoring Magna, Snoring Parva, Tatterford, Tattersett, Thursford, Toftrees and West Barsham. £19.95.

Vol.7. Billockby, Burgh St Margaret, Caister-on-Sea, East Somerton, Filby, Hemsby, Oby, Ormesby St. Margaret, Ormesby St. Michael, Oby & Ashby, East and West Somerton. £19.95.

Vol.8. Doughton, East Rudham, Helhoughton, Horningtoft, Little Massingham, Shereford, South Creake, Syderstone, Waterden, West Rudham and Whissonett. £19.95.

Vol.9. Castle Rising, Congham, Flitcham, Gaywood, Grimston, Hillington, North Wootton, Roydon and South Wootton. £19.95.

Vol.10. Leziate, East Walton, East Winch, Gayton, Gayton Thorpe, Great Massingham, Middleton, Pentney, Westacre, and West Bilney. £19.95.

Vol.11. East Rainham, North Runcton, South Rainham, Swaffham, and West Rainham. £19.95.

Vol.12. Anmer, Bagthorpe, Barwick, Bircham Newton, Bircham St Mary, Bircham Tofts, Dersingham, Southmere, Ingoldisthorpe, Sedgeford, Shernborne, Southmere and Stanhow, with Barwick. £19.95.

Norfolk 1817 poll book. £19.95.

Northamptonshire

Northamptonshire Phillimore parish records (marriages).
Originally published 1908- . 2 CDs. Contents:

Vol. 1. Castor, Dodford, Faxton, Glinton, Heyford, Northborough, Peakirk, Stoke Bruerne, Weston by Welland, & Sutton Bassett. £19.95.

Vol. 2. Croughton, Everdon, Farthingstone, Harpole, Lamport, Northampton St. Peter, & Stowe Nine Churches. £19.95.

Northamptonshire 1823 Pigot's directory. £5.95.

Northumberland

Northumberland poll book 1826. £19.95.
Newcastle. Byker 1891 census. £19.95.

Nottinghamshire

Nottinghamshire Phillimore parish records (marriages). 22 CD's. £19.95 per CD. Or all 22 vols. on 1 CD, £438.90. Forthcoming. Contents:

Vol.1. Bingham, Car Colston, East Bridgford, Elton on the Hill, Flintham, Granby, Hawksworth, Kneeton, Nottingham (St.Mary), Orston, Scarrington, Screveton, Whatton. £19.95.

Vol.2. Broughton Sulney, or Over Broughton, Colston Bassett, Cotgrave, Cropwell Bishop, Hickling, Kinoulton, Holme Pierrepoint, Owthorpe, Radcliffe on Trent, Shalford, Tithby, Tollerton. £19.95.

Vol.3. Bolderton, Barnby, Coddington, Cotham, East Stoke, Newark Castle, Elston Chapelry, Elston, Farndon. £19.95.

Vol.4. Flawborough, Hawton, Kilvington, Shelton, Sibthorpe, Staunton, Staunton Chapel, Syerston, Thorpe juxta Newark, Winthrope, Newark. £19.95.

Vol.5. Costock, Gotham, Kingston on Soar, Normanton on Soar, Rempston, West Leake, East Leake, Stanford on Soar, Sutton Bonington (St. Michael's), Widmerpool. £19.95.

Vol.6. Attenborough, Basford, Beeston, Bramcote, Lenton. £19.95.

Vol.7. Willoughby on the Wolds, Wysall, Barton in Farbis, Thrumpton, Ratcliffe on Soar, West Bridgford, Ruddington, Clifton, Wilford, Edwalton, Keyworth. £19.95.

Vol.8. Cossall, Trowell, Stapleford, Strelley, Wollaton, Nuttall, Awsworth, Greasly. £19.95.

Vol.9. Radford, Hucknall Torkard, Annesley, Bulwell, Bunny, Langar. £19.95.

Vol.10. Snenton, Colwick, Gedling, Burton Joyce, Lowdham. £19.95.

Vol.11. Eastwood, Selston, Sutton in Ashfield, Kirkby in Ashfield, Skegby, Teversal. £19.95.

Vol.12. Lambley, Woodborough, Calverton, Epperston, Oxton, Goralston, Hoveringham, Thurgarton, Tithby (additional). £19.95.

Vol.13. Arnold, Mansfield Woodhouse, Mansfield, Sutton in Ashfield. £19.95.

Vol.14. Mansfield. £19.95.

Vol.15. Newark. £19.95.

Vol.16. Southwell, Bleasby, Halloughton, Marton, Upton. £19.95.

Vol.17. Rolleston cum Fiskerton, Averham, Kelham, Hockerton, Caunton, Maplebeck, South Muskham, North Muskham, Holme, Plumtree, Stanton on the Wolds. £19.95.

Vol.18. Blidworth, Farnsfield, Kirklington, Edingley, Halam, Askham, Beckingham, Laneham. £19.95.

Vol.19. Langford, South Collingham, North Collingham, South Scarle, Girton, North Clifton, Thorney. £19.95.

Vol.20. Winkburn, Kneesall, Norwell, Cromwell, Ossington, Sutton on Trent, Weston, Normanton on Trent, Marnham, Fledborough.

Nottingham. Headon baptisms, marriages and burials 1566-1812. Originally published Parish Register Society **43**. 1902. £19.95.

Oxfordshire

Oxfordshire Phillimore parish records (marriages). Originally published 1909-10. 2 CD's. Contents:

Vol. 1. Chipping Norton, Wootton, Pyrton, Crowell. £19.95.

Vol. 2. Eynsham, Stanton Harcourt, Standlake, Hanborough, Northmoor, Yarnton, Cassington. £19.95.

Oxfordshire 1823 Pigot's directory. £19.95.

Oxfordshire 1844 Pigot's directory. £19.95.

S & N Genealogy Supplies (*continued*)
Pembrokeshire
Pembrokeshire records 1066-1994. Various records including calendar of public records, hearth tax 1670, Pennar baptisms, Castle Martin Hundred, Haverfordwest 1539-1660 and various publications by Basil Hughes. £24.95.

Rutland
Rutland. North Luffenham baptisms, marriages and burials 1572-1812. Originally published Parish Register Society **4**. 1896.

Shropshire
Shropshire. Battlefield 1665-1812. Originally published Parish Register Society **4**. 1899. £19.95.

Shropshire. Clunbury parish registers. Originally published Parish Register Society **38**. 1901. £19.95.

Shropshire. Cressage baptisms, marriages and burials 1605-1812. Originally published Parish Register Society **27**. 1900. £19.95

Shropshire. Ford 1589-1812. Originally published Parish Register Society **29**. 1900. £19.95.

Shropshire. Harley baptisms, marriages and burials 1745-1812. Originally published Parish Register Society **23**. 1899. £19.95.

Shropshire. Hopton Castle baptisms, marriages and burials 1538-1812. Originally published Parish Register Society **40**. 1901. £19.95.

Shropshire. Hughley baptisms, marriages and burials 1576-1812. Originally published Parish Register Society **41**. 1901. £19.95.

Shropshire. Melverley baptisms, marriages and burials 1723-1812. Originally published Parish Register Society **24**. 1899. £19.95.

Shropshire. More baptisms, marriages and burials 1569-1812. Originally published Parish Register Society **34**. 1900. £19.95.

Shropshire. Pitchford baptisms, marriages and burials 1558-1812. Originally published Parish Register Society **31**. 1900. £19.95.

Shropshire. Selattyn baptisms, marriages and burials 1557-1812. Originally published Parish Register Society **58**. 1906. £19.95.

Shropshire. Sheinton baptisms, marriages and burials 1658-1812. Originally published Parish Register Society **28**. 1900. £19.95.

Shropshire Shipton baptisms, marriages and burials, 1538-1812. Originally published Parish Register Society **22**. 1899. £19.95.

Shropshire. Sibdon Carwood 1538-1812. Originally published Parish Register Society **20**. 1899. £19.95.

Shropshire. Smethcote baptisms, marriages and burials 1605-1812. Originally published Parish Register Society **26**. 1899. £19.95.

Shropshire. Stapleton baptisms, marriages and burials 1546-1812. Originally published Parish Register Society **35**. 1901. £19.95.

Somerset

Somerset Phillimore parish records (marriages). Originally published in 15 vols., 1898-1915. 15 CD's. £19.95 per CD. Or all 15 vols. on 1 CD, £149.63. Contents:

Vol.1. Aller, Charlton Adam, Charlton Mackrell, High Ham, Huish Episcopi, Kingsdon, Long Sutton, Muchelney, Northover and Langport. £19.95.

Vol.2. Pitney, Limington, Podymore Milton, Somerton, Yeovilton, North Curry and Barrow Gurney. £19.95.

Vol.3. Curry Rivel, Drayton, Long Load, Martock and West Hatch. £19.95.

Vol.4. Ashill, Isle Brewer, Beer Crocombe, Ilton, Whitestaunton, Stocklinch Magdalen, Stocklinch Ottersay, Barrington, Shepton Beauchamp, Buckland St. Mary, Wraxhall, Puckington and Swell. £19.95.

Vol.5. Crewkerne, Fivehead, Kingsbury Episcopi and Swell. £19.95.

Vol.6. Aisholt, Broomfield, Charlynch, Dodington, Durleigh, Enmore, Otterhampton, Overstowey, Stockland Gaunts, Cannington, and Spaxton. £19.95.

Vol.7. Angersleigh, Pitminster, Corfe, Orchard Portman, Stoke St Mary, Thurlbear, Trull, Creech St Michael and Bradford. £19.95.

Vol.8. Hill Farrance, Heathfield, Thorne Faulcon, West Monkton, Ruishton, West Buckland, Cothelstone, Ash Priors, Norton Fitzwarren, Cheddon Fitzpaine, Langford Budville, Nynehead. £19.95.

Vol.9. Taunton (St. Mary Magdalene). £19.95.

Vol.10. Taunton (St. Mary Magdalene). £19.95.

Vol.11. Wellington, Ashbrittle, Runnington, Otterford, Sampford Arundel and Thorne St. Margaret. £19.95.

Vol.12. Stogursey, Nether Stowey, East Quantoxhead, Fiddington, Goathurst, Chedzoy, Kilve, Crowcombe, Thurloxton, Stringston, Kilton and Lilstock. £19.95.

Vol.13. Staple Fitzpaine, Bickenhall, Lopen, Whitelackington, Hinton St. George, Ilminster and Milverton. £19.95.

Vol.14. Combe St. Nicholas, West Bagborough, Isle Abbots, Kittisford, Kilmington, East Pennard, Midsomer Norton and Weston-Super-Mare. £19.95.

Somersetshire 1844 Pigot's directory. £19.95.

Bath. The registers of Bath Abbey 1569-1800. Originally published Harleian Society registers **27-8.** 1900-1. £19.95.

Bath & Wells bishops transcripts / E. Dwelly. Originally published 1913-14. 2 CD's (A-H & H-Y). £19.95 per CD. Earliest B.T's only.

Bath & Wells bishops transcripts part 3 / E. Dwelly. Originally published 1915. £19.95. Covers Abbas Combe, Aisholt, Alford, Aller, Allerton, Almsford, Argersleigh, Ashbrittle, Ashcott, & Ashill, 1597-1811.

Bath & Wells bishops transcripts part 4 / E. Dwelly. Originally published 1917. £19.95. Covers Ansford, 1807, Ash Priors, Ashington, Ashwick, Axbridge, Babcary, Babbington, Backwell, Badgworth, South Barrow, c.1595-1813; Wrington, 1806-7.

S & N Genealogy Supplies (*continued*)

Bath & Wells bishops transcripts part 5 & 6 / E. Dwelly. Originally published 1919. £19.95. Covers Bath parishes of St. James, St. Peter, St. Paul, & St. Michael; also Widcombe & Ottery.

Suffolk

Suffolk Phillimore parish records (marriages). Originally published 1910-31. 4 CD's. £19.95 per CD.

    Vol. 1. Thrandeston, Exning, Little Wenham, Martlesham, Capel St. Mary, Combs, Great Wenham. £19.95.

    Vol. 2. Woodbridge. £19.95.

    Vol. 3. Hoxne, Syleham, Mendham, Metfield, Withersdale. £19.95.

    Vol. 4. Fressingfield, Weybread, Somerleyton, Ashby, Risby, Dunwich St. Peter, Grundisburgh, Mickfield, Thrandeston. £19.95.

Suffolk 1823 Pigot's directory. £5.95.

Suffolk. Ipswich St. Nicholas: baptisms, marriages & burials 1539-1710. Originally published Parish Registers Society 7. 1897. £19.95.

Suffolk. West Stow and Wordwell registers: baptisms, marriages, burials & inscriptions to 1850. Originally published 1903. £19.95.

Surrey

Surrey parish records. All items listed below on 1 CD, £169.57.

Surrey parish records, vol.1. Richmond 1583-1720. Originally published 1903. £19.95.

Surrey parish records, vol.2. Godalming 1582-1688. Originally published 1904. £19.95.

Surrey parish records, vol.3. Richmond 1720-1780. Originally published 1905. £19.95.

Surrey parish records, vol.4. Farleigh, Tatsfield, Warborough and Woldingham. Originally published 1906. £19.95.

Surrey parish records, vol.5. Addington, Chelsham, and Warlingham. Originally published 1907. £19.95.

Surrey parish records, vol.6. Gatton & Sanderstead. Originally published 1908. £19.95.

Surrey parish records, vol.7. Chipstead & Titsey. Originally published. 1909. £19.95.

Surrey parish records vol.8. Coulsdon & Haslemere 1594-1772. Originally published 1910. £19.95.

Surrey parish records, vol.9. Stoke D'Abernon & Haslemere 1772-1812. Originally published 1915. £19.95.

Surrey parish records, vol.11. Putney 1620-1734. Originally published 1913. £19.95.

Surrey parish records vol.12. Putney 1735-1812. Originally published [191-?] £19.95.

Surrey parish records vol.13. Putney banns & marriages 1774-1870. Originally published 1916. £19.95.

Surrey parish records vol.14 & 15. Caterham 1543-1837. Originally published 1917-18. £19.95.

Surrey parish records. Extra vol.1. Merstham. Originally published 1902. £19.95.

Surrey. Banstead 1547-1789. Originally published Parish Register Society 1. 1896. £19.95.

Surrey. Morden baptisms, marriages & burials 1634-1812.
Originally published Parish Register Society **37**. 1901.
£19.95.

Surrey 1823 Pigot's directory. £15.95.

Sussex

Sussex 1820 pollbook. £19.95.

Sussex 1823 Pigot's directory. £19.95.

Warwickshire

Warwickshire Phillimore parish records (marriages). 3 CD's.
£19.95. per CD. Contents:

Vol.1. Fenny Compton, Bourton on Dunsmore, Long
Compton, Anstey, Leamington Priors, Priors Hardwick,
Whitchurch, Atherstone on Stour, Idlicote, Temple
Grafton, Butters Marston, Ettington, Honington, Long
Compton. £19.95.

Vol.2. Birmingham (Franciscan register of St. Peter's,
baptisms). £19.95.

Vol.3. Birmingham (Franciscan register of St. Peter's),
Bishop's Tachbrooke, Charlecote, Halford, Snitterfield,
Hatton, Barton on the Heath. £19.95.

Warwickshire. Rowington 1612-1812. Originally published
Parish Register Society **21**. 1899. £19.95.

*Warwickshire. Stratford-on-Avon Holy Trinity marriages 1558-
1812.* Originally published Parish Register Society **16**. 1898.
£19.95.

Warwickshire. Stratford-on-Avon baptisms 1558-1653.
Originally published Parish Register Society **6**. 1897. £19.95.

Wiltshire

Swindon 1915 voters list. £19.95.

Wiltshire 1844 Pigot's directory. £5.95.

Wiltshire Phillimore parish records (marriages). 14 CD's.
£19.95 per CD. Or all 14 vols. on 1 CD, £139.65.

Vol.1. Mere, Monkton Deverill, Kingston Deverill, Sherston
Magna, Alderton, Sopworth, Grittleton, and Leigh
Delamere. £19.95.

Vol.2. Marlborough - St Peter's & St Mary's, Yatton Keynell,
and Durrington. £19.95.

Vol.3. East Knoyle, Britford, Ashley, Crudwell, Stockton,
Long Newnton, Milston, Bulford, Newton Tony,
Allington, and Boscombe. £19.95.

Vol.4. Preshute, Urchfont, Stert, and Colerne. £19.95.

Vol.5. Baverstock, Colerne, Norton, and Salisbury St
Thomas. £19.95.

Vol.6. Castle Eaton, Kemble, Great Somerford, Southbroom,
Patney, Cherington/Chirton, Marden, Alton Barnes,
Winterslow, and Rollestone. £19.95.

Vol.7. Salisbury Cathedral, Purton, Charlton, and Huish.
£19.95.

Vol.8, Beechingstoke, Chisledon, Idmiston, Lydiard
Millicent, Lavington, Minety, Porton, and Woodborough.
£19.95.

Vol.9. Salisbury St Martin. £19.95.

Vol.10. Laverstock, Hankerton, Brinkworth, Malford, Clyffe
Pypard, Heytesbury, Knook, Eisey, and West Knoyle.
£19.95.

S & N Genealogy Supplies (*continued*)
    Vol.11. Whiteparish, Devizes, and Luckington. £19.95.
    Vol.12. Bratton, Kington St Michael, Fuggleston St Peter,
       Bemerton, Boyton, Sherrington, and Latton, and
       Collingbourne Ducis. £19.95.
    Vol.13. Salisbury St Edmund. £19.95.
    Vol.14. Salisbury St Edmund, Stratford-Sub-Castle. £19.95.

Worcestershire
Worcestershire 1842 Pigot's directory. £19.95.
Worcestershire Phillimore parish records (marriages). 2 CD's.
    £19.95 per CD. Contents:
    Vol.1. Shipston-on-Stour, Tidmington, Bradley, Kempsey,
       Alderminster, Offenham, Alstone, Kington, Redditch,
       Church Lench, Rous Lench and Elmbridge. £19.95.
    Vol.2. North Littleton, Middle Littleton, South Littleton,
       Churchill-in-Halfshire, North Piddle, Himbleton,
       Huddington, Cleeve Prior, Little Comberton, Upton
       Snodsbury, Bushley, Birtsmorton, Rushock, Frankley,
       Eastham, Orleton and Hanley William. £19.95.
Worcestershire. Worcester St. Albans. 1630-1812. Originally
    published Parish Register Society 2. 1896. £19.95.

Yorkshire
Yorkshire. Phillimore parish records (marriages). Originally
    published 1914-15. 4 CD's. £19.95 per CD. Contents:
    Vols.1-2. Rotherham. (2 CDs).
    Vols.3-4. Doncaster (St.George). (2 CDs).
*Yorkshire. Adel baptisms, marriages, burials and inscriptiosn
1606-1812.* Originally published Thoresby Society 5. 1895.
    £19.95.
*Yorkshire. Blacktoft baptisms, marriages and burials 1700-
1812.* Originally published Yorkshire Parish Register
    Society 8. 1900.
*Yorkshire. Burton Fleming or North Burton baptisms,
marriages and burials 1538-1812.* Originally published
    Yorkshire Parish Register Society 2. 1899.
*Yorkshire. Cherry Burton baptisms, marriages and burials
1561-1740.* Yorkshire Parish Register Society 15. 1903.
*Yorkshire. Darrington St. Luke & All Saints baptisms,
marriages and burials 1567-1812.* Originally published
    Yorkshire Parish Register Society 49. 1913.
Yorkshire. Garforth baptisms, marriages and burials 1631-1812.
    Originally published Yorkshire Parish Register Society 46.
    1913. £19.95.
Yorkshire. Gargrave baptisms, marriages and burials 1558-1812.
    Originally published Yorkshire Parish Register Society 28.
    1907. £19.95.
*Yorkshire. Hackness baptisms, marriages and burials 1557-
1783.* Originally published Yorkshire Parish Register
    Society 25. 1906. £19.95.
*Yorkshire. Harewood baptisms 1614-1812, and marriages 1621-
1812.* Originally published Yorkshire Parish Register
    Society 50. 1914. £19.95.
Yorkshire. Huggate baptisms, marriages and burials 1539-1812.
    Originally published Parish Register Society 36. 1901.
    £19.95.

Yorkshire. Kirk Ella baptisms, marriages and burials 1558-1841. Originally published Parish Register Society **11**. 1897. £19.95.

Yorkshire. Kirklington baptisms, marriages and burials 1568-1812. Originally published Yorkshire Parish Register Society **35**. 1909. £19.95.

Yorkshire. Parish church of Leeds. Baptisms, marriages and burials 1619-1695. Originally published Thoresby Society 3(2), 7 & 10. 1895-1901. £19.95.

Yorkshire. Marske in Cleveland baptisms, marriages and burials 1569-1812. Originally published Yorkshire Parish Register Society **16**. 1903. £19.95.

Yorkshire. Monk Fryston baptisms, burials and marriages, 1538-1687. Originally published Parish Register Society **5**. 1896. £19.95.

Yorkshire. Otley part 1. Baptisms, marriages and burials 1562-1672. Originally published Yorkshire Parish Register Society **33**. 1908. £19.95.

Yorkshire. Saxton-in-Elmet baptisms, marriages and burials 1538-1812. Originally published Yorkshire Parish Register Society **93**. 1932. £19.95.

Yorkshire. Scorborough baptisms, marriages and burials 1700-1812. Originally published Yorkshire Parish Register Society **8**. 1900. £19.95.

Yorkshire. Settrington baptisms, marriages and burials 1559-1812. Originally published Yorkshire Parish Register Society **38**. 1910.

Yorkshire. Snaith pt. II. Burials 1537-1656. Originally published Yorkshire Parish Register Society **63**. 1919. £19.95.

Yorkshire. Terrington baptisms, marriages and burials 1599-1812. Originally published Yorkshire Parish Register Society **29**. 1907.

Yorkshire. York St. Martin, Coney Street, baptisms, marriages and burials 1557-1812. Originally published Yorkshire Parish Register Society **36**. 1909. £19.95.

Yorkshire. York, Goodramgate, baptisms, marriages and burials 1573-1812. Yorkshire Parish Register Society **41**. 1911. £19.95.

Yorkshire. Pickhill cum Roxby baptisms, marriages, and burials 1567-1812. Originally published Yorkshire Parish Register Society **20**. 1904. £19.95.

Yorkshire. Topcliffe and Morley baptisms 1654-1830, and burials 1654-1888. Originally published 1888. £19.95.

Sheffield general and commercial directory 1821. £19.95.

Wales

Wales (North and South) 1844 Pigot's directory. £19.95.

Wales. South and West Wales genealogical index: marriages, censuses and wills (Carmarthen and Pembroke). £29.95. 160,000 entries.

K.G.Saur

Ortlerstrasse 8, D-8000 Munchen 70, Germany
Webpage: www.saur.de

World Biographical index. 7th ed. DM1,980.00. Includes data on 2,800,000 people worldwide, including text from 592 British biographical dictionaries.

Scottish Genealogy Society

Sales Secretary, 15 Victoria Terrace, Edinburgh, EH1 2JL, Scotland.
Email: info@scotsgenealogy.com
Webpage: www.scotsgenealogy.com

Retours of services of heirs, 1544-1699. £32.00.
Services of heirs in Scotland, 1700-1859. £37.00. This and the preceding CD record the inheritance of lands in Scotland.
The Scots peerage / Sir James Balfour Paul. Originally published in 9 vols., 1904-14. £60.00.

Sgian Dhu Interactive

20, Somerville Drive, Mount Florida, Glasgow, Scotland G42 9BQ.
Email: info@sgiandhu.com

The clans and tartans of Scotland on CD-Rom. £29.95. History of the Scottish clans system.
Tartan for Windows. £9.99. Guide to nearly 500 tartan designs.

Shelkay

c/o Richard W. Townsend, F.R.Ae.S., Cornwall Legacy, Windrush, Crofton Avenue, Lee-on-the-Solent, PO13 9NJ.
Phone/Fax: 01329 668 938
Email: CornwallLegacy@aol.com
Webpage: Cornwall-Legacy.com

Nonconformist registers for Cornwall held at the Public Record Office: Methodist & Independent records 1760-1851. £29.95 + p&p (U.K.) £2.50. Transcript. Also available in book format.
North Hill parish registers held mainly at the Cornwall Record Office, 1555-1900. £29.95 + p&p (U.K.). Transcript. Also available in book format.
Cornish Quaker records. Forthcoming.

Wm. Frank Skidmore

267, Golf Course Lane, Winchester, Tennessee, 37398, U.S.A.
Email: skidwf@earthlink.net
Website: www.skidmoregenealogy.com

System Requirements
Please specify Macintosh or PC when ordering

Skidmore genealogy. $US75.00. Family history in England and America.

Stepping Stones

P.O.Box 295, York, YO31 1YS.
Phone: (01904) 424131
Fax: (01904) 422351
Email: judd@mjudson.freeserve.co.uk
Webpage: www.stepping-stones.co.uk

Prices

Add p&p £1.50 for the first CD; 50p for each additional CD.
Overseas p&p: USA £2.75; Europe £2.25; Australia £3.00

Principal cities 1822 trade directory. £11.99. Contents:
Birmingham, Bristol, Coventry, Kidderminster, Kilmarnock, Leicester, Liverpool, London, Macclesfield, Manchester.

Bristol
Bristol directory 1852/3. £11.99.

Cambridgeshire
Cambridgeshire directory 1830. £11.99.

Cheshire
Pigots Cheshire 1828-29 trade directory. £11.99.

Cornwall
Kelly's 1919 trade directory for Cornwall. £11.99.

Cumberland
Cumberland directory 1834. £11.99.

Devon
Pigot's Devonshire 1830 trade directory. £11.99.

Durham
Pigot's 1834 trade directory for Durham and surrounding villages. £11.99.

Essex
Pigot's 1832-3 trade directory. £11.99.

Hampshire
Hampshire directory 1830. £11.99.

Herefordshire
See Northamptonshire

Kent
Kent directory 1832-3-4. £11.99.

Lancashire
Lancashire 1848 trade directory. £11.99.
Slater's Liverpool 1848 trade directory. £11.99.
Slater's Manchester 1848. £11.99.

Lincolnshire
Lincolnshire directory 1876. £11.99. Forthcoming.

London & Middlesex
Middlesex directory 1839. £11.99.
Kelly's London 1865 trade directory, part 1. £11.99. List by trades
Kelly's London 1865 trade directory part 2. £11.99. List by trade
Kelly's London 1865 commercial directory part 1. £11.99. Alphabetical names and addresses of commercial trades people, A-K.

Stepping Stones (*continued*)

Kelly's London 1865 commercial directory part 2. £11.99.
Alphabetical names and addresses of commercial trades
people, H-Z.

London street directory 1865 part 1. £11.99. Contents: Abbey
Gardens to Knightsbridge Green.

London street directory 1865 part 2. £11.99. Haberdashers
Place East to Young Street.

Norfolk
Norfolk directory 1830. £11.99.

Northamptonshire
*Northamptonshire directory 1841, and Herefordshire directory
1835.* £11.99.

Northumberland
Pigot's 1822 trade directory for Northumberland. £11.99.
Northumberland directory 1848. £11.99.
Newcastle and Gateshead 13th & 14th century journal. £11.99.
Contents: Month by month journal of events 1301-1500,
mentioning names of new land owners, inn leaseholders,
deeds, wills, *etc., etc.* £11.99.

Nottinghamshire
Nottingham directory 1854. £11.99.

Oxfordshire
Oxfordshire directory 1830. £11.99.

Shropshire
Slater's Shropshire 1858/59 trade directory. £11.99.

Somerset
Somersetshire directory 1851. £11.99.

Staffordshire
Staffordshire directory 1828/29. £11.99.

Suffolk
Suffolk directory 1840. £11.99.
Suffolk directory 1883. £11.99. Forthcoming.

Surrey
Surrey directory 1840. £11.99.

Sussex
Sussex directory 1832-33-34. £11.99.

Wiltshire
Slater's Wiltshire 1851 trade directory. £11.99.

Worcestershire
Worcestershire directory 1828-29. £11.99.

Yorkshire
Illustrated Yorkshire churches. £11.99.
*White's trade directory for the East Riding 1822, including
Hull.* £11.99.
*North Yorkshire directory 1822, including Scarborough &
Whitby.* £11.99.
Baines 1822 trade directory for the West Riding. £11.99.
*Kelly's 1872 Post Office directory for the East Riding of
Yorkshire.* £11.99.

Kelly's 1872 North & East Riding of Yorkshire. £11.99.
Kelly's 1897 residents directory for the East Riding of Yorkshire. £11.99.
Kelly's 1897 street & trade directory for North Yorkshire. £11.99.
Kelly's 1897 North & East Riding of Yorkshire court & profession directory. £11.99.
Kelly's 1897 trade directory for Hull & surrounding villages. £11.99.
Leeds 1853 street & trade directory. £11.99.
Leeds street directory 1907. £11.99. Forthcoming.
1902 street & trade directory for Scarborough, Whitby, Filey & surrounding villages. £11.99.
Sheffield town centre 1822 trade directory. £11.99.
White's trade directory for York & Ainsty 1822. £11.99.
Kelly's 1897 street & trade directory for York, including York inns, now with added photos. £11.99.

Scotland
Directory of Edinburgh & Leith 1848. £11.99.
Glasgow directory 1838/39. £11.99.

Wales
Pigot's North Wales, 1828-9, & South Wales, 1830. £11.99.

Stuart Tamblin
See Family History Indexes

T.W.R.Computing
Clapstile Farm, Alpheton, Sudbury, Suffolk, CO10 9BN.
Phone: 01284 828271
Email: sales@twrcomputing.co.uk
Webpage: www.twrcomputing.co.uk

Agents for a number of CD publishers

Marleen Van Horne
423 So. 12th Street, San Jose, CA., 95112-2231, U.S.A.
Email: msvnhrn@jps.net
Webpage: www.jps.net/msvnhrn

History of the Mathesons. Forthcoming. Scottish Family.

Wartime Research Media
P.O.Box 5611, Brentwood, CM14 5TW.
Phone: (01277) 201613
Fax: (01277) 201615
Email: info@wartime-research.com

Murphy's register. Forthcoming. Contents: 50,000 photographs of men and women who served in the 1st World War.

H.W.Wilson Company

950 University Avenue, Bronx, NY 10452, U.S.A.
Webpage: www.hwwilson.com

Biography index. Price on application. Regular updates.
Indexes biographical material from over 3000 current
periodicals.

Wilson biographies. Price on application. Annual updates.
Biographical information on 72,000+ people.

Current biography. Price on application. Regular updates.
Over 14,000 biographies and 8,900 obituaries which have
appeared since 1940.

Wiltshire Index Service

11 Ardmore Close, Gloucester, GL4 OBJ.
Email: wis@cwcom.net
Webpage: www.wis.mcmail.com

1871 census surnames, Wiltshire. £19.95 + p&p. Includes
surname, place, piece no., folio reference, LDS film
references. Also published in 22 volumes on fiche.

Wilson-Trace Wiltshire burials index (collection 1). £19.95 +
p&p. Indexes 125,000 burials. Also available on 2 fiche.

Wiltshire wills beneficiaries index (1800-1858). Collection 1.
£19.95. Index to wills from 14 peculiar courts (over 1,000
wills). Also available on 8 fiche.

Wolverhampton Archives and Local Studies

42-50, Snow Hill, Wolverhampton, West Midlands WV2 4AG.
Phone: 01902 552480
Fax: 01902 552481
Email: wolverhamptonarchives@dial.pipex.com
Website: www.wolverhampton.gov.uk/archives

Bilston in the 19th century. £9.99. Extracts from trade
directories, 1818, 1834, 1851, 1872, & 1896; cholera map 1832;
6" Ordnance Survey map 1885.

Subject Index

Counties are indicated in accordance with the
Chapman system of county codes.

Parish Registers (*continued*)

Awsworth (Ntt) 73
Axbridge (Som) 75
Aycliffe (Dur) 53
Ayleston (Lei) 20, 70
Aylestone (Lei) 69
Babbington (Som) 75
Babcary (Som) 75
Babingly (Nfk) 71
Backwell (Som) 75
Badgworth (Som) 75
Badlesmere (Ken) 46
Baggrave (Lei) 20
Bagthorpe (Nfk) 72
Ballast Hills (Nbl) 52
Banstead (Sry) 76
Barkby (Lei) 14, 20, 69
Barkston (Lei) 20, 69
Barley (Hrt) 68
Barnby (Ntt) 73
Barrington (Som) 75
Barrow Gurney (Som) 75
Barrow on Soar (Lei) 20, 70
Barrow on Trent (Dby) 12, 65
Barrowby (Lin) 70
Barton in Farbis (Ntt) 73
Barton on the Heath (War) 77
Barton Turf (Nfk) 72
Barwick (Nfk) 72
Basford (Ntt) 73
Basing (Ham) 67
Basingstoke (Ham) 67
Bassingham (Lin) 70
Bath (Som) 75, 76
Batsford (Gls) 67
Battlefield (Sal) 74
Baughurst (Ham) 67
Baverstock (Wil) 77
Bawsey (Nfk) 71
Beaconsfield (Bkm) 62
Beaminster (Dor) 66
Beauchief (Dby) 12, 65
Beckingham (Ntt) 73
Bedingham (Nfk) 72
Beeby (Lei) 14, 20, 70
Beechingstoke (Wil) 77
Beer Crocombe (Som) 75
Beer Hackett (Dor) 65
Beesby (Lin) 70
Beeston (Ntt) 73
Beighton (Dby) 12, 65
Belgrave (Lei) 20, 70
Belton (Lin) 45
Bemerton (Wil) 78
Benenden (Ken) 46
Bentley (Ham) 68
Bentworth (Ham) 68
Berkshire 62
Berrington (Hrt) 68
Beverston (Gls) 67
Bickenhall (Som) 75
Biddenden (Ken) 46

Billockby (Nfk) 72
Bilsby (Lin) 70
Bingham (Ntt) 72
Bircham Newton (Nfk) 72
Bircham St.Mary (Nfk) 72
Bircham Tofts (Nfk) 72
Birmingham (War) 77
Birstall (Lei) 20, 70
Birtsmorton (Wor) 78
Bisham (Brk) 62
Bishop Middleham (Dur) 53
Bishop's Cleeve (Gls) 66
Bishop's Tachbrooke (War) 77
Bishopton (Dur) 53
Bishopwearmouth (Dur) 53
Bitteswell (Lei) 20, 69
Bitton (Gls) 67
Blaby (Lei) 20, 70
Blacktoft (Yks) 78
Blanchland (Nbl) 53
Bleasby (Ntt) 73
Blidworth (Ntt) 73
Blisland (Con) 10, 63
Bodmin (Con) 11, 63
Bolderton (Ntt) 73
Boldon (Dur) 53
Boldre (Ham) 68
Boothby Graffoe (Lin) 70
Booton (Nfk) 71
Boscombe (Wil) 77
Bosley (Chs) 63
Bothenhampton (Dor) 66
Bottesford (Lei) 14, 20, 69
Botus Fleming (Con) 11, 64
Boughton under Blean (Ken)
  46
Boultham (Lin) 70
Boulton (Dby) 12, 64
Bourton on Dunsmore (War)
  77
Bourton on the Water (Gls) 67
Boxted (Ess) 66
Boxwell (Gls) 67
Boxworth (Cam) 62
Boyton (Con) 11, 64
Boyton (Wil) 78
Bracebridge (Lin) 70
Bradenham (Bkm) 62
Bradfield (Brk) 62
Bradford (Som) 75
Brading (Ham) 68
Bradley (Wor) 78
Bradpole (Dor) 66
Brailsford (Dby) 12, 65
Bramcote (Ntt) 73
Bramley (Ham) 67
Brancepeth (Dur) 53
Branston (Lei) 20, 69
Bratton (Wil) 78
Braunston (Lei) 20, 70
Braydeston (Nfk) 71
Breadsall (Dby) 12, 65

Dorchester. Holy Trinity (Dor) 66
Dorney (Bkm) 62
Dorset 66
Dorsington (Gls) 66
Doughton (Nfk) 72
Drayton (Som) 75
Drayton Parslow (Bkm) 62
Dronfield (Dby) 12, 65
Dry Drayton (Cam) 62
Duffield (Dby) 12, 65
Duke Place. St.James (Lnd) 71
Dunham Magna (Nfk) 71
Duntisbourne Abbots (Gls) 67
Duntisbourne Rous (Gls) 67
Dunwich St. Peter (Sfk) 76
Durham 52
Durham. Cathedral (Dur) 53
Durham. St.Margaret (Dur) 53
Durham. St.Mary le Bow (Dur) 53
Durham. St.Mary South Bailey (Dur) 53
Durham. St.Nicholas (Dur) 53
Durham. St.Oswald (Dur) 53
Durleigh (Som) 75
Durrington (Wil) 77
Dursley (Gls) 67
Eagle (Lin) 70
Easington (Dur) 53
East Allington (Lin) 70
East Barsham (Nfk) 72
East Bridgford (Ntt) 72
East Chelborough (Dor) 66
East Knoyle (Wil) 77
East Leake (Ntt) 73
East Peckham (Ken) 46
East Pennard (Som) 75
East Quantoxhead (Som) 75
East Rainham (Nfk) 72
East Rudham (Nfk) 72
East Somerton (Nfk) 72
East Stoke (Ntt) 73
East Stour (Dor) 66
East Sutton (Ken) 46
East Walton (Nfk) 72
East Winch (Nfk) 72
Eastham (Wor) 78
Eastington (Gls) 67
Eastrop (Ham) 67
Eastwell (Lei) 14, 20, 70
Eastwick (Hrt) 68
Eastwood (Ntt) 73
Eaton (Lei) 20, 69
Ebchester (Dur) 53
Edgworth (Gls) 67
Edingley (Ntt) 73
Edlesborough (Bkm) 62
Edmonton (Mdx) 71
Edmundbyers (Dur) 53
Edwalton (Ntt) 73
Egglecliffe (Dur) 53

Egloshayle (Con) 10, 63
Egloskerry (Con) 10, 63
Eisey (Wil) 77
Eling (Ham) 68
Elkstone (Gls) 67
Elmbridge (Wor) 78
Elston (Ntt) 73
Elston Chapelry (Ntt) 73
Elstree (Hrt) 68
Elsworth (Cam) 62
Eltisley (Cam) 62
Elton on the Hill (Ntt) 72
Elvaston (Dby) 12, 65
Elvetham (Ham) 67
Elwall (Dby) 12, 65
Elwick Hall (Dur) 53
Embleton (Dur) 53
Endellion (Con) 10, 63
Enfield (Mdx) 71
Enmore (Som) 75
Epperston (Ntt) 73
Epworth (Lin) 45
Escombe (Dur) 52
Esh (Dur) 53
Essex 66
Ettington (War) 77
Everdon (Nth) 15, 72
Eversley (Ham) 67
Evington (Lei) 14, 20, 69
Ewhurst (Ham) 68
Exning (Sfk) 76
Eye Kettleby (Lei) 20
Eynsford (Ken) 68
Eynsham (Oxf) 73
Faccombe (Ham) 67
Fairfield (Dby) 12, 65
Fairford (Gls) 67
Fakenham (Nfk) 72
Falmouth (Con) 11
Farleigh (Sry) 76
Farlesthorpe (Lin) 70
Farnborough (Ham) 67
Farndon (Ntt) 73
Farnsfield (Ntt) 73
Farthingstone (Nth) 15, 72
Faxton (Nth) 15, 72
Feltham (Mdx) 71
Fen Drayton (Cam) 62
Fenny Compton (War) 77
Fiddington (Som) 75
Filby (Nfk) 72
Filton (Gls) 67
Finchley (Mdx) 71
Fingest (Bkm) 62
Fiskerton (Ntt) 73
Fivehead (Som) 75
Flawborough (Ntt) 73
Fledborough (Ntt) 73
Fleet (Dor) 66
Fleet (Lin) 70
Flintham (Ntt) 72
Flitcham (Nfk) 72

Hawridge (Bkm) 62
Hawton (Ntt) 73
Haxey (Lin) 45
Hayes (Mdx) 71
Heacham (Nfk) 71
Headon (Ntt) 73
Heanor (Dby) 12, 65
Heath (Dby) 12, 64
Heathery Cleugh (Dur) 53
Heathfield (Som) 75
Heckfield (Ham) 67
Heckington (Lin) 70
Hedenham (Nfk) 72
Hedgerley (Bkm) 62
Hedsor (Bkm) 62
Hedworth (Dur) 53
Heighington (Dur) 53
Helhoughton (Nfk) 72
Helland (Con) 10, 63
Helston (Con) 11, 64
Hemblington (Nfk) 71
Hemsby (Nfk) 72
Henbury (Gls) 67
Herriard (Ham) 68
Herringby (Nfk) 72
Hertfordshire 68
Heston (Mdx) 71
Hetton le Hole (Dur) 53
Heworth (Dur) 53
Hexham (Nbl) 54
Heyford (Nth) 15, 72
Heytesbury (Wil) 77
Hickling (Nfk) 72
Hickling (Ntt) 72
High Ham (Som) 75
High Wycombe (Bkm) 62
Highclere (Ham) 68
Hill (Gls) 67
Hill Farrance (Som) 75
Hillingdon (Mdx) 71
Hillington (Nfk) 72
Himbleton (Wor) 78
Hinton on the Green (Gls) 66
Hinton St.George (Som) 75
Histon (Cam) 62
Hitcham (Bkm) 62
Hoby (Lei) 14, 20, 69
Hockerton (Ntt) 73
Hogsthorpe (Lin) 70
Holbeach (Lin) 44
Holkham (Nfk) 71
Hollingbourne (Ken) 46
Holme (Ntt) 73
Holme by the Sea (Nfk) 72
Holme Hale (Nfk) 72
Holme Pierrepoint (Ntt) 72
Holwell (Lei) 20
Honington (War) 77
Hook (Dor) 66
Hopton Castle (Sal) 74
Hormead (Bkm) 62
Horningtoft (Nfk) 72

Horsley (Dby) 12, 65
Horsley (Gls) 67
Horstead (Nfk) 71
Horton (Gls) 67
Horton (Nbl) 53
Hose (Lei) 20, 69
Hoton (Lei) 14, 20, 70
Houghton le Spring (Dur) 53
Houghton on the Hill (Lei) 20
Hounslow (Mdx) 71
Hove (Ssx) 17
Hoveringham (Ntt) 73
Hoxne (Sfk) 76
Hucknall Torkard (Ntt) 73
Huddington (Wor) 78
Huggate (Yks) 78
Hughendon (Bkm) 62
Hughley (Sal) 74
Huish Episcopi (Som) 75
Hull (Yks) 43
Humberstone (Lei) 14, 20, 70
Hungerton (Lei) 14, 20, 70
Hunstanworth (Dur) 53
Huntingdonshire 68
Huntley (Gls) 67
Hurstbourne Priors (Ham) 67
Hurstbourne Tarrant (Ham) 67
Hurworth (Dur) 53
Huttoft (Lin) 70
Hyde (Ham) 68
Ibstone (Bkm) 62
Ickenham (Mdx) 71
Icombe (Gls) 67
Idlicote (War) 77
Idmiston (Wil) 77
Ilkeston (Dby) 12, 65
Ilminster (Som) 75
Ilton (Som) 75
Impington (Cam) 62
India 55
Ingersby (Lei) 20
Ingoldisthorpe (Nfk) 72
Ingoldmells (Lin) 70
Ingworth (Nfk) 71
Ipplepen (Dev) 65
Ipswich (Sfk) 76
Ireland 55
Isle Abbots (Som) 75
Isle Brewer (Som) 75
Iver (Bkm) 62
Ivinghoe (Bkm) 62
Jacobstow (Con) 11, 64
Jarrow (Dur) 53
Jarrow Grange (Dur) 53
Kea (Con) 11, 64
Keadby (Lin) 45
Kedleston (Dby) 12, 65
Kelham (Ntt) 73
Kelloe (Dur) 53
Kemble (Wil) 77
Kemerton (Gls) 66
Kempsey (Wor) 78

Pitminster (Som) 75
Pitney (Som) 75
Pitstone (Bkm) 62
Pittington (Dur) 53
Plumtree (Ntt) 73
Plungar (Lei) 21, 69
Plymouth (Dev) 65
Podymore Milton (Som) 75
Popham (Ham) 68
Porton (Wil) 77
Portsmouth. St.Thomas (Ham) 68
Portsmouth. St.Thomas a Becket (Ham) 68
Pott Shrigley (Chs) 63
Poughill (Con) 11, 64
Poundstock (Con) 11, 64
Powerstock (Dor) 66
Poynton (Chs) 63
Preshute (Wil) 77
Prestbury (Chs) 63
Prestbury (Gls) 67
Preston (Dor) 66
Preston (Ssx) 17
Preston Candover (Ham) 68
Preston upon Stour (Gls) 66
Prestwold (Lei) 14, 21, 70
Priors Hardwick (War) 77
Probus (Con) 11, 64
Puckington (Som) 75
Purley (Brk) 62
Purton (Wil) 77
Putney (Sry) 76
Pyrton (Oxf) 73
Quarndon (Dby) 12, 65
Quedgeley (Gls) 66
Quenby (Lei) 20
Queniborough (Lei) 14, 21, 70
Quinton (Gls) 67
Quorndon (Lei) 14, 21, 70
Radcliffe on Trent (Ntt) 72
Radford (Ntt) 73
Ragdale (Lei) 14, 21, 69
Rame (Con) 24
Rampisham (Dor) 66
Ramsey (Hun) 68
Ranworth (Nfk) 71
Ratby (Lei) 14, 21, 69
Ratcliffe on Soar (Ntt) 73
Ratcliffe on the Wreak (Lei) 14, 21, 70
Rearsby (Lei) 14, 21, 70
Redditch (Wor) 78
Redmarshall (Dur) 53
Redmile (Lei) 21, 69
Redruth (Con) 11, 64
Rempston (Ntt) 73
Rendcombe (Gls) 66
Repton (Dby) 12, 65
Richmond (Sry) 76
Rickmansworth (Hrt) 68
Rigsby (Lin) 70

Risby (Sfk) 76
Risley (Dby) 12, 64
River (Ken) 46
Roche (Con) 11, 64
Rolleston (Lei) 73
Rollestone (Wil) 77
Rotherby (Lei) 14, 21, 69
Rotherham (Yks) 78
Rotheswick (Ham) 68
Rothley (Lei) 21, 70
Rous Lench (Wor) 78
Rowington (War) 77
Rowner (Ham) 68
Roxby (Yks) 79
Roxwell (Ess) 66
Roydon (Nfk) 72
Ruan Lanyhorne (Con) 11, 64
Ruan Major (Con) 11, 64
Ruan Minor (Con) 11, 64
Ruddington (Ntt) 73
Ruishton (Som) 75
Runham (Nfk) 72
Runnington (Som) 75
Rushock (Wor) 78
Ryton (Dur) 53
Saint Agnes (Con) 11, 64
Saint Allen (Con) 11, 64
Saint Antholin. Budge Row (Lnd) 40
Saint Anthony in Meneage (Con) 11, 64
Saint Breock (Con) 11, 64
Saint Breward (Con) 10, 63
Saint Buryan (Con) 10, 63
Saint Cleer (Con) 10, 63
Saint Clement (Con) 11, 64
Saint Clether (Con) 10, 63
Saint Colan (Con) 11, 63
Saint Columb Major (Con) 11, 64
Saint Columb Minor (Con) 11, 64
Saint Cubert (Con) 11, 64
Saint Dennis (Con) 11, 64
Saint Dionis Backchurch (Lnd) 71
Saint Dominick (Con) 24
Saint Enoder (Con) 11, 64
Saint Erme (Con) 11, 64
Saint Erney (Con) 11, 64
Saint Erth (Con) 11, 64
Saint Ervan (Con) 11, 64
Saint Eval (Con) 11, 64
Saint Ewe (Con) 11, 63
Saint Germans (Con) 24
Saint Germoe (Con) 10, 63
Saint Gluvias (Con) 11, 63
Saint Gorran (Con) 11, 63
Saint Hilary (Con) 11, 63
Saint Issey (Con) 11, 64
Saint Ives (Con) 11, 24, 64
Saint John's Chapel (Dur) 53

Somerton (Som) 75
Sopley (Ham) 68
Sopworth (Wil) 77
Soulbury (Bkm) 62
South Barrow (Som) 75
South Collingham (Ntt) 73
South Creake (Nfk) 72
South Croxton (Lei) 14, 21, 70
South Hykeham (Lin) 70
South Kelsey. St.Mary (Lin) 70
South Kelsey. St.Nicholas (Lin) 70
South Littleton (Wor) 78
South Mimms (Mdx) 71
South Muskham (Ntt) 73
South Perrot (Dor) 66
South Petherwin (Con) 11, 64
South Rainham (Nfk) 72
South Scarle (Ntt) 73
South Shields (Dur) 53
South Warnborough (Ham) 67
South Westoe (Dur) 53
South Wingfield (Dby) 12, 65
South Wootton (Nfk) 72
Southacre (Nfk) 71
Southbroom (Wil) 77
Southmer (Nfk) 72
Southmere (Nfk) 72
Southrop (Gls) 67
Southwell (Ntt) 73
Spalding (Lin) 70
Sparsholt (Brk) 62
Spaxton (Som) 75
Spondon (Dby) 12, 65
Staindrop (Dur) 52
Stalbridge (Dor) 66
Standish (Gls) 67
Standlake (Oxf) 73
Stanford on Soar (Ntt) 73
Stanhope (Dur) 53
Stanhow (Nfk) 72
Stanley (Dby) 12, 64, 65
Stanton (Gls) 66
Stanton by Bridge (Dby) 12, 65
Stanton by Dale (Dby) 12, 64
Stanton Harcourt (Oxf) 73
Stanton on the Wolds (Ntt) 73
Stanwell (Mdx) 71
Staple Fitzpaine (Som) 75
Stapleford (Lei) 14, 21, 70
Stapleford (Lin) 70
Stapleford (Ntt) 73
Staplehurst (Ken) 68
Stapleton (Sal) 74
Stathern (Lei) 21, 69
Staunton (Ntt) 73
Staunton Chapel (Ntt) 73
Stert (Wil) 77
Steventon (Ham) 67
Stinchcombe (Gls) 66, 67
Stockland Gaunts (Som) 75
Stocklinch Magdalen (Som) 75

Stocklinch Ottersay (Som) 75
Stockton (Wil) 77
Stogursey (Som) 75
Stoke Abbot (Dor) 66
Stoke Bruerne (Nth) 15, 72
Stoke D'Abernon (Sry) 76
Stoke Poges (Bkm) 62
Stoke St.Mary (Som) 75
Stone (Bkm) 62
Stone (Gls) 66
Stonehouse (Gls) 66
Stoughton (Lei) 21
Stourmouth (Ken) 46
Stowe Nine Churches (Nth) 15, 72
Stratfield Turgis (Ham) 67
Stratford on Avon (War) 77
Stratford Sub Castle (Wil) 78
Strathfieldsaye (Ham) 67
Stratton (Con) 11, 64
Strelley (Ntt) 73
Stringston (Som) 75
Strubby (Lin) 70
Strumpshaw (Nfk) 71
Stubton (Lin) 70
Stythians (Con) 10, 63
Suffolk 76
Sulham (Brk) 62
Sunbury (Mdx) 71
Sunderland (Dur) 53
Surfleet (Lin) 70
Surrey 76
Sutton Bassett (Nth) 15, 72
Sutton Bonington (Ntt) 73
Sutton in Ashfield (Ntt) 73
Sutton le Marsh (Lin) 70
Sutton on Trent (Ntt) 73
Sutton Poyntz (Dor) 66
Sutton under Brailes (Gls) 66
Sutton Valence (Ken) 46
Swaffham (Nfk) 72
Swalecliffe (Ken) 47
Swarkeston (Dby) 12, 65
Swavesey (Cam) 62
Swell (Som) 75
Swinderby (Lin) 70
Swindon (Gls) 66
Swithland (Lei) 14, 21, 70
Swyre (Dor) 66
Syde (Gls) 67
Syderstone (Nfk) 72
Syerston (Ntt) 73
Syleham (Sfk) 76
Symondsbury (Dor) 66
Sysonby (Lei) 20
Syston (Lei) 14, 21, 70
Tadley (Ham) 67
Tangley (Ham) 67
Taplow (Bkm) 62
Tarrant Hinton (Dor) 65
Tatsfield (Sry) 76
Tatterford (Nfk) 72

Author Index

Surname Index

Place Name Index

Lancashire (*continued*)

Liverpool 26, 39, 55, 81
Liverpool. Everton 32
Lune Valley 48
Manchester 7, 14, 26, 81
Oldham 26
Ormskirk 26
Padiham 69
Preston 26
Rochdale 26
Saint Helens 26
Salford 10, 14, 26
Scotforth 48
Southport 26
Todmorden 26
Ulverston 26
Warrington 26
Whalley 26
Wigan 26, 69
Wittington 69

Lancashire, North 48

Leicestershire 14, 16, 30, 31, 40, 47, 55, 69

Ab Kettleby 14, 20, 69
Asfordby 20, 70
Ashby de la Zouch 26
Ashby Folville 14, 70
Ashby Parva 20, 69
Ashford Folville 20
Ashfordby 14
Ayleston 20, 70
Aylestone 69
Baggrave 20
Barkby 14, 20, 69
Barkston 20, 69
Barrow on Soar 20, 70
Beeby 14, 20, 70
Belgrave 20, 70
Birstall 20, 70
Bitteswell 20, 69
Blaby 20, 70
Bottesford 14, 20, 69
Branston 20, 69
Braunston 20, 70
Brentingby 14, 21, 70
Brooksby 14, 20, 69
Burrough on the Hill 20, 69
Burton Lazars 20, 69
Burton on the Wolds 21
Bushby 70
Caldwell 70
Calthorpes 69
Castle Donnington 26
Catthorpe 20
Caudwell 21
Cold Newton 20, 70
Congerston 14, 20, 69
Cossington 14, 20, 70
Coston 14, 20, 69
Cotes 21
Cropston 70
Croxton Kerrial 20, 69
Eastwell 14, 20, 70
Eaton 20, 69
Evington 14, 20, 69
Eye Kettleby 20
Freeby 20, 69

Frisby on the Wreak 14, 20, 69
Frolesworth 20, 69
Gaddesby 14, 20, 69
Gilmorton 20, 69
Glen Parva 20, 70
Glenfield 20, 70
Goadby Marwood 14, 20, 70
Great Dalby 20, 69
Grimston 14, 20, 70
Harby 20, 69
Harston 20, 69
Hinckley 26
Hoby 14, 20, 69
Holwell 14, 20, 69
Hose 20, 69
Hoton 14, 20, 70
Houghton on the Hill 20, 70
Humberstone 14, 20, 70
Hungerton 14, 20, 70
Ingersby 20
Keyham 20, 70
Kirby Bellars 14, 20, 69
Kirby Muxloe 20, 70
Knighton 20, 70
Knipton 20, 69
Leicester 26, 47, 81
Leire 20, 69
Little Dalby 20
Long Clawson 14, 20, 70
Loughborough 26
Lowesby 20, 70
Lubbesthorpe 20, 70
Lutterworth 26
Market Harborough 26
Market Rasen 26
Melton Mowbray 20, 26, 69
Mountsorrel 20, 70
Muston 14, 20, 69
Nether Broughton 14, 20, 70
Newbold Saucey 14, 20, 70
Old Dalby 14, 20, 70
Owston 14, 20, 70
Pickwell 21, 69
Plungar 21, 69
Prestwold 14, 21, 70
Quenby 20
Queniborough 14, 21, 70
Quorndon 14, 21, 70
Ragdale 14, 21, 69
Ratby 14, 21, 69
Ratcliffe on the Wreak 14, 21, 70
Rearsby 14, 21, 70
Redmile 21, 69
Rolleston 73
Rotherby 21, 69
Rothley 21, 70
Saxby 14, 21, 70
Saxelbye 14, 70
Scalford 14, 21, 69
Scraptoft 14, 21, 69
Seagrave 14, 21, 70
Sharnford 21, 69
Sholeby 14, 70
Sibson 14, 21, 69
Sileby 14, 21, 70
Somerby 14, 21, 69
South Croxton 14, 21, 70
Stapleford 14, 21, 70